urban
canada

second edition revised

james and robert simmons

Copp Clark Publishing
A Division of Copp Clark Limited
Vancouver   Calgary   Toronto   Montreal

ISBN 0 7730 3201 0

29, 122

Copp Clark Publishing
517 Wellington Street West
Toronto M5V 1G1

Printed and bound in Canada.

contents

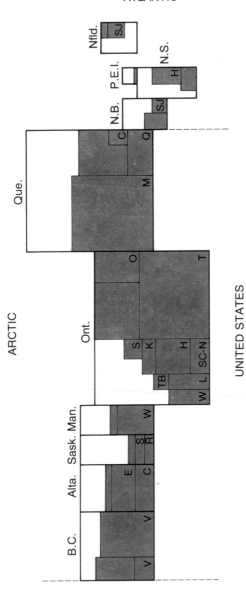

ATLANTIC

ARCTIC

PACIFIC

UNITED STATES

Area Proportional to Population

Data obtained from Statistics Canada, *Census of Canada, 1971*.

Census metropolitan areas

Other urban areas over 10,000

1 Canada is an Urban Nation

"... Canadians have flocked to cities, but
their institutions, their habits of mind, and
especially, perhaps, their mythology, have
lagged behind.

The jut-jawed outdoorsman, still vivid
against a prairie sky, a rocky coastline or
a stand of black spruce, still works long
hours as a national symbol. To a degree,
this is very well: such people exist, and
their race will, we profoundly trust, en-
dure, providing a flesh-and-blood link
with the pioneer past. But the unromantic
fact is that most Canadians today are not
like this at all. They live and work in
cities and towns; their environment, for
most of the year at least, is an urban and
largely man-made one."

Royal Commission on Canada's
Economic Prospects
(The Gordon Commission),
Final Report, 1957

1

The Changing Image

What is your image of Canada? Bald prairie sweeping to bleak horizons? The crumpled rocks and straggly pines of the Shield? An Arctic waste stretching across the top of a continent? The image may be true of the vast expanse of Canada's physical landscape, but as the quotation on page 1 points out, it has very little to do with the lives of most Canadians.

The real Canadian scene is a cityscape: smooth pavements and squared-off walls, crowds of people at lunch-time, flowing night-time expressways, and miles of houses elbowing each other. Canadians and their activities are becoming more and more concentrated in a hundred or so urban areas which occupy less than one per cent of the land area.

Gone are the occupations linked to the soil, the rock, and the timber. Canadians are stenographers, dentists, school teachers, salesmen. They depend, not on nature and their own brute strength, but on massive organizations which affect most aspects of their existence. They struggle—more or less— against the giant corporations which employ them, the bank that determines the interest rates on their mortgages, or the city hall which decides the amount of schooling, street washing and parking they may have. Canadians live in close contact with their fellows in a complex, varied, man-made environment called the city. It generates new problems, new solutions, new life-styles.

The traditional map of Canada with its enormous pastel provinces and tiny dots of cities is not much help in describing Canada in the late twentieth century. The broad sweeping patterns of the distribution of resources which show up on such maps are less relevant, economically, socially and politically, than the intense variations which take place within the few miles separating city and country, or even the few blocks between different social areas of the city. An accurate map of most of the socioeconomic variables describing Canada would show a few dozen islands of intense activity and great variation, separated by hundreds of miles of low density, homogeneous areas.

If we consider people, rather than rocks and trees, the map of Canada looks much like the frontispiece. The twin metropolises of Montreal and Toronto dominate the country. They generate more production and interaction than any of the provinces except their own. Together they represent 6.3 million people, almost thirty per cent of the population, and produce 40 per cent of the gross national product within less than one hundredth of one per cent of the area of Canada. Montreal, Toronto and the other hundred or so cities of Canada provide the day-to-day surroundings, the jobs, the homes, for over two-thirds of all Canadians. One apartment block contains the population of hundreds upon hundreds of square miles of prairie.

But it is not enough to realize the significance of the urban fact in Canadian life. We must take a good look at the urban environment—the surroundings which shape our lives, control our comforts, make our living. Understanding of what a city is, how it comes to be, the processes by which it grows and changes, is the first step toward improving the quality of Canadian life.

And as we study the Canadian city all the larger issues of Canadian life are reproduced in miniature. Problems of growth, of regional disparity, of allocation of political power, of conflicts between culture groups exist within urban areas. Often they are more visible, more clearly understood in the context of a single urban area. The differences between rich and poor are greater and more clearly defined within the cities of Winnipeg or Sherbrooke than between the provinces of British Columbia and New Brunswick. Toronto and Montreal thrust more diverse cultural groups into daily contact than does all the rest of Canada. Are the grumblings of a prairie farmer and a small-town French-Canadian as they read their respective newspaper editorials really as relevant to the country as a whole as the daily cross-cultural experiences in a Montreal office or on a Toronto street car?

The Emergence of an Urban Way of Life

It is time we began to look at Canada as an urban phenomenon. The concentration of Canadians into urban areas, and the resulting changes in their way of life have been going on since before the first white settlement. When Champlain and his men wintered at Port Royal in 1605, The Order of Good Cheer was an urban organization. For that matter, Cartier found that Hochelaga (now Montreal) was a well-developed Indian town in 1534 with twenty apartment buildings (long-houses) and a municipal government. Long before Confederation there was a difference between the backwoods boy and the storekeeper's son, between Sam Slick and his rural customers.

But it is in the last twenty-five years that the urban way of life has become predominant, and strikingly evident. The first generation raised in an urban environment is now beginning to reproduce. Their children are wholly urban. Streets, stores, subways, and apartment buildings compose their environment. Outside of cats and dogs, the only animals they see are at racetracks, or in zoos, or on television. The trees and flowers are planted in rows, and the snow is cleared away as it falls.

Although urban life appears to be a fixture, there are still those who say that we leave the natural (i.e. rural) environment at great cost to our psyche. The individual is overwhelmed by the scale of urban life, the thousands of people who do exactly the same thing each day, or who live in identical apartments and work shoulder to shoulder on assembly lines. The price of economic opportunity is the loneliness that may result when a person knows only a small part of other peoples' lives.

But others point out the advantages of urban life: the increased productivity, leading to higher living and health standards and more leisure; the intellectual stimulation and economic rewards of specialized jobs; the diversity of recreational opportunities; the wide range of daily social contacts; the permissiveness which allows one to live one's own life. In a city one can design cars, devote one's life to rare coins, or become a specialist in diseases of the larynx. On a given evening, even in Flin Flon or Sorel, half a dozen activities will be in process: Parent-Teacher Associations, service clubs, a couple of movies, a hockey game, curling, bridge. City-dwellers can become Christian Scientists or New Left activists, take mistresses or take pot, wear kilts or overalls, and find friends to applaud their taste.

The diversity of activities, of jobs, of people and neighbourhoods, is common to all urban areas and is one of the main characteristics which differentiate them from the non-urban. Sociologists stress the amount of personal interaction in urban life—the number and variety of people and activities actually encountered each day—and the many different roles which a city-dweller assumes: bus driver, lodge member, parent and soccer fan. Each role means involvement with different people in different locations, and with different organizations operating under different rules. If a spouse or boss make some roles unpleasant, there is always someone else to swear at or to talk to.

It is the fact of the cities' continuing ability to attract people and activities from non-urban areas that most effectively repudiates any myth of the inherent superiority of rural life. People come to the cities because they want to. Urban

5

life is appealing: to the teenager who needs places to hang out with other teenagers, to the young technician or clerk who wants to switch jobs or take night-classes, and to the working-class housewife who likes to be in daily contact with all her female kinfolk. The larger the city, the easier it is to provide stores and services in an immigrant's own language, and to serve the people with special problems: the unwed mothers, the alcoholics, or the retarded.

Yet the rural-urban differences are rapidly disappearing as urban areas expand. Most of the variations in attitudes stem from differences in the age distribution of rural and urban populations and from differences in social class and ethnic origin. The generation gap rather than differences in the rural and urban environments separates the two. In rural and small-town areas, many of the people in the 20-to-35 age group have moved to the city. Urban areas have a disproportionate number of young people.

If these demographic factors are controlled, much of the distinction between rural and urban behaviour disappears. Many of the values and attitudes of the young college-trained farmer are indistinguishable from those of his urban cousin in advertising. Both are tanned from winter vacations in the south, both watch the same television channels, read the same newspapers, cheer the same hockey team and drink the same beer. The supermarkets they patronize are identical and the hardware stores they visit sell the same lawn lounges, with nails, pickaxes and barbed wire relegated to the back of the store. Differences between rural and urban areas decline as one or the other becomes dominant. A hundred years ago the whole nation was concerned with rural problems and adopted rural attitudes; now the urban life-style and urban mores reach and rule all parts of the country.

This is the real meaning of "Urban Canada". As the urban environments predominate, and urban life-styles become more extensive, all parts of Canada become more "urban".

Decisions of economic and social policy, such as the allocation of government funds to various programmes, or the control and direction of education, are made by politicians raised in an urban environment, serving an urban constituency, living an urban life. The mass media, reaching into every remaining farm and fishing village, originate in the big cities and represent urban points of view, showing urban landscapes, amenities, events.

The most highly urbanized and centralized economic activities are those of decision-making. Business corporations, governments, and universities require an urban setting. In a few blocks along Bay Street or St. James Street decisions are made about private investments which modify a landscape a thousand miles away. No wonder the prairie farmer distrusts the Bay Street barons, but so does the suburban mortgage-seeker. The citizen also feels threatened by civil servants in Ottawa or Fredericton, who plan programmes of taxes, services and development which affect almost every aspect of his daily life: what he learns in school, what he can afford to buy, whether there will be more parks or more highways.

The city exists to provide these intense, productive, highly specialized interactions among people, but it also shapes the decisions that result. The urban environment filters the information people have about other places; it selects, by availability, the people who are consulted; it modifies all goals and values to serve urban interests. Can the executive of an international corporation based in Montreal, where there are thousands of alternative industries, really comprehend the impact of a decision to close the only factory in a town in Nova Scotia? Could he ever bring himself to transfer his executives and their families to Swift Current, Saskatchewan? Does the advertising expert really try to communicate with the people in Cornerbrook, Newfoundland, or Rimouski, Quebec, or is it easier to make them over in his own image?

7

Defining "Urban" Places

In order to define precisely what we mean by urban
Canada, we shall have to use demographic criteria such as size
or density of population. There is an implication of particular
forms of behaviour as well. We expect that most urban persons
will not derive their income directly from agriculture; their
economic activities will differ from those of rural Canadians,
and their patterns of social interaction, their priorities—social,
economic and political—may differ.

By 1971 over 75 per cent of Canadians were categorized
as urban according to Statistics Canada. This means that they
lived in cities, towns, villages, or unincorporated settlements
of greater than 1,000 persons, or in the built-up fringes
(population density greater than 1,000 per square mile) of
incorporated areas of over 50,000 people. The level of urbanization increases still more if we add the 18% of the Canadian population who are officially living outside urban areas
but are classed as non-farm, meaning they do not earn a
living from agriculture. Many of them are commutors, driving
into nearby cities and towns for work and recreation. Of the
remaining 1.5 million who are farm residents (7 per cent of
the population) the majority live within fifty miles of a city.
By any of these arbitrary locational classifications, Canada is
overwhelmingly an urban nation.

If we are to look closely at Canada's urban nature, however, a more useful but equally arbitrary line must be drawn to
differentiate cities from non-urban areas. The problem is not
an easy one. The size threshold separating urban and rural
varies in different countries because of cultural differences. In
Canada every town of over 1,000 people is called urban, while
in the United States the minimum size is 2,500 and in other
countries 10,000 or more. But all of these size thresholds are
far below what many people would call a city. They would

apply the term only to populations of 100,000 or more, the point when specialized land uses and social groups clearly sort themselves out.

Much of the conceptual confusion seems to arise from the psychological and cultural factors of personal experience. The meaning of "urban" tends to depend on the degree of urbanity of the user. To a native New Yorker, no other place in the world is truly urban. A Torontonian may grudgingly admit the existence of Montreal, but he will not grant the urbanity of places like Portage la Prairie or even Ottawa.

Similarly, the time and place are important influences in determining the sense of what is urban. The 4,000 people of Montreal in 1750 dominated the economic and social life of half a continent, and considered themselves truly urban, yet what rural figures those people would have cut in Paris. Today, Yellowknife has a population of only 6,000 yet acts as the urban focal point of the whole of Northwest Canada. Towns of similar size in Southern Ontario or Quebec, such as Ingersoll or Iberville, can scarcely pretend to the same urban status. There is an international sense of "urban" as well, correlating with the level of economic progress and sophistication. By all these criteria, too, Canada is urban.

In this book we shall use two basic levels of urbanity which seem to be most useful in differentiating Canadian urban places. First, we shall concern ourselves only with those places of over 10,000 population (116 of them) which we shall call cities. And secondly, we shall pay particular attention to the twenty-two cities of over 100,000 which are defined by Statistics Canada as Census Metropolitan Areas. These we shall call simply Metropolitan Areas. They are listed, with some of their statistical characteristics, in the appendix.

The other definitional problem is to draw a physical limit around an urban area. It is increasingly difficult to tell where the city stops and the country begins. Each city presents new problems. How far north does Montreal extend? Are

9

1.1 The North American Urban System

Data obtained from Statistics Canada, *Census of Canada, 1971*, and
United States Bureau of the Census, *Census of Population, 1970*.

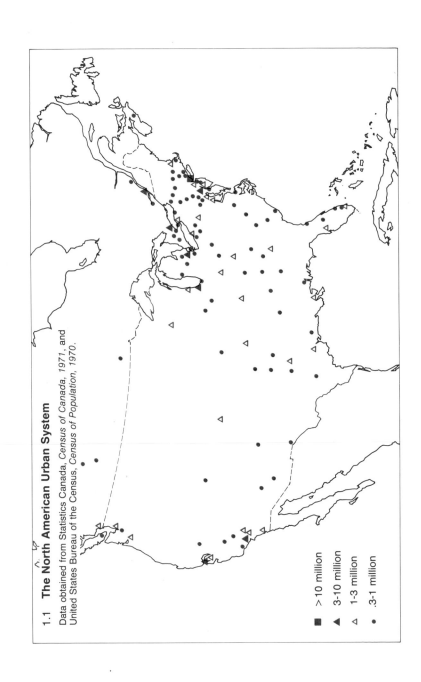

■ >10 million

▲ 3-10 million

△ 1-3 million

• .3-1 million

Halifax and Dartmouth really one city? Does Niagara Falls become a larger place just because annexation changes the official boundaries? Several metropolitan areas now have two-tier governments, the municipality and a regional authority: Which is the real Ottawa? Urban analysts have used a wide variety of criteria to decide these questions, including political boundaries, density measures, the degree of social and economic contact among neighbouring communities, and combinations of all of these. We will use Statistics Canada's metropolitan definitions where possible, and cities' political boundaries in other cases.

The census taker includes as a metropolitan area "an incorporated city of at least 50,000 persons, which with surrounding built-up areas comprises an urbanized core of at least 100,000 persons. In addition those rural areas are included which are within a half-hour driving time of the core. The total is defined as the main labour market."

Canadian and American Cities

Urban Canada has both much in common with the cities of the United States and many differences from them. Innumerable books, magazine articles and television shows have examined U.S. cities and their problems. The accumulated research on American cities and the varied experience of Americans in coping with urban problems give insight into processes currently taking place in Canada such as urban growth and obsolescence, transportation and housing crises.

Canadian and American cities are alike in that their urban areas absorb virtually all of a high rate of national growth; in the fact of the automobile, the personal transportation system; and in the recognition of the role of private enterprise in urban development. As we shall see, each of these factors affects the kinds of urban problems and solutions which we face. It is the similarity in these three areas which makes the American experience more relevant to Canadians than urban life in Britain or Sweden. The pressures of growth, the traffic jams and the aesthetic horrors perpetrated in the name of the market economy—all originated, and will have to be studied and solved, on this side of the ocean.

At the same time Canadian urban areas differ significantly from U.S. cities for a variety of reasons. Solutions applicable to American cities must be carefully evaluated before they can be fully accepted here. The major areas of difference are the mixture of ethnic origins, the institutional patterns, and the recent historical record.

Many modern American cities are hampered in some ways by racial antagonisms. The rapidly growing black population in the central city accentuates the traditional conflict between city and suburbs and the urban-rural battles in the state legislature. Every expressway, every new school, every housing project or urban renewal programme can become a source of racial controversy. Whites resist any proposal which would permit the negro community to expand spatially. Blacks fight for their own priorities in public spending.

In Canadian cities the ethnic pattern is more varied and less easily linked to urban decisions. Many cities are predominantly of either French or British descent and even in those cities with large numbers of New Canadians the problems of mutual cultural adjustment are not easily associated with urban growth and development programmes. The sources of dissatisfaction and stress are therefore varied and complex, difficult to identify and generalize. Many of the Canadian immigrants are already middle-class, white-collar families who disappear rapidly into the suburbs. Others, of half a dozen different national origins, are upwardly mobile, often achieving considerable economic success within a few years. They obscure

12

the poverty, exploitation and acculturation difficulties of the remainder. Only when the successful and unsuccessful newcomers become sorted out, economically, socially and spatially, will these problems play a significant role in urban policy.

At present many middle- and upper-class Canadians still see the centre of a city as an attractive place to live. Residential land costs near downtown are increasing rapidly, generating a large amount of private redevelopment. Old houses are repainted and sold as townhouses at astronomical prices. Expensive apartment buildings spring up everywhere. New capital is flowing into stores and offices in all parts of the central city.

In comparable U.S. cities, despite massive infusions of federal urban renewal funds, city centres are in difficulty. The expansion of the low-income, low-buying-power black ghettos near the central business district leads to a decline in the number of stores, and difficulties in attracting private capital. Public expenditures on public housing, urban renewal or expressways displace residents of older neighbourhoods. Middle-class families with children flee to the suburbs and the sheltered school systems.

Canadian cities also differ institutionally from their American counterparts. Particularly significant is the relatively small role played by the federal government in the redevelopment of urban areas. Canada has not undertaken major federal programmes in urban renewal, public housing or expressway construction. Our programmes in these activities tend to be smaller and more dependent on local initiative.

The province, on the other hand, controls almost every aspect of municipal institutions, using its powers freely to reorganize city government, change boundaries and run school systems. In the United States, where traditions of local autonomy are still strong, such things are just not done. In Canada each province tends to standardize aspects of urban life controlled by the public sector. A significant source of standardization in most provinces is the strong planning legislation which gives the municipality considerable power to determine the physical form of the city if it wishes to do so. An equally important Canadian characteristic is the rapid expansion of municipal political boundaries, whether by annexation or by some form of metropolitan government. Costs of growth or blight are shared by all areas of the city. In the U.S. with its differing traditions, the tendency is to develop ring after ring of small independent suburban governments around the central city.

Finally, the recent histories of Canada and the U.S. have differed significantly. Canada continued in the depth of economic depression until the Second World War began in 1939. The depression, the war, and the post-war recovery period held public investment at a very low level for almost twenty years. The U.S. economy on the other hand had begun to revive in the late thirties and early forties, thanks in part to a major public works programme. Public investment in slum clearance and public housing was initiated at that time and the automobile way of life was firmly established even before the rapid rise in incomes due to the war.

Post-war Canada had a great backlog of basic services to supply in housing, roads, schools and parks. The need for quantity, coupled with the lower Canadian standard of living, slowed down the rate of innovation. The surge of automobile ownership and the low-density city came later here. Canadian cities have been slower to develop shopping plazas and expressways. The ubiquitous air conditioning, the downtown composed of parking lots, the endless sprawl of subdivisions and gas stations are not quite at the same stage yet in Canada. Despite its equivalent growth rate, Toronto is not Los Angeles; we cannot quite afford the high-horsepower cars and the network of expressways which make the *completely* decentralized city possible. Recently, too, Canadians have indicated that they may not wish to follow the same path even if they can afford it. The lag provides time for reconsideration.

14

Exploring the Urban Environment

For all its importance, urban Canada is still largely unexplored. This is the true frontier; a man-made environment so complex that its effects on our way of life seem unpredictable; a man-created world that man seemingly cannot control. The city grows to unbounded size and towards some unknowable final form while politicians and planners tunnel through it, attempting to explore it, trying to patch up small portions of it.

It is arguable whether we shall ever know enough about cities to plan them completely. But it is worthwhile to try to understand this urban environment that surrounds us, to try to comprehend the often confusing and ugly landscape, to try to appreciate the variety of man's largest artifact.

We can profit from investigating the great differences among cities—variations which provide as rich a choice of environments as is found in the natural landscape. Compare the streets and buildings of Edmonton and Halifax; the looks and preferences of people in Victoria and Trois Rivières; the physical backdrops to Vancouver and Sudbury. Canadian cities, so few and so diverse, create vivid and unique impressions. Let the names roll off your tongue and the images flash through your mind: Chicoutimi, Saskatoon, Nanaimo. They stimulate powerful responses—local loyalties to St. John's or Calgary, or the secret envy all other Canadians feel for Montrealers.

Even the simplest criteria indicate the enormous variations among the cities of Canada. The size varies: Midland has 11,000 inhabitants; Montreal has 2.7 million. The age varies: Quebec was founded in 1608; Kitimat and Thompson mushroomed from nothing in the early 1950's. The economy varies: one-third of the male labour force of Timmins works in the mines; in Ottawa these men would all be bureaucrats.

Within the individual city, the diversity is even more marked, creating a variety of environment and experience which a rural landscape cannot rival. The cityscapes change abruptly within a few blocks. The crowded cliffs of downtown turn to desolate wooden warehouses by the docks. Neon signs and noise surround a tree-hung park and fountains. Decaying single-story dwellings are overlooked by giant luxury apartments, while beyond them lies a quiet ravine with streams and secret paths and sunshine straying down through layered leaves. Life in Toronto's Cabbagetown differs more from life in the mansions of Rosedale, only a mile away, than Newfoundland differs from Saskatchewan. Even in the smaller cities the variety is there, in a more compressed form. The growing end of Main Street, with the latest doctor's office and the new beauty parlour, contrasts with the area by the tracks with its dowdy restaurant, milk bar and bus station.

Urban alternatives are numerous: the tension of downtown, the placidity of the suburbs, the anonymity of the highrise apartment or of skid row. And as new cultures emerge in the urban environment—the Italians, the intellectuals, the middle-class swingers, the hippies, the homosexuals—they, too, lay claim to a part of the city and mark it off as their own.

But, study of the urban environment becomes possible because of the basic similarities. Cities do have patterns in common. We can observe regularities in the activities of the inhabitants as they work, plan, build, make decisions. The locations, timing and results of these actions can be examined. A kind of common "urban-life" may be projected for all city-dwellers, with standard sets of occupations, life-styles and traffic jams. The pattern of the visible urban landscape contains basic similarities for all centres too. Experienced city-dwellers know where to look for a bar or a pawnshop, and when the rush hour starts on Fridays.

We shall generalize about these regularities of form and of behaviour. Many are valid for virtually every city, others true only for Canada, or for different regions in Canada. Many of the regularities, such as the size and shape and combinations of stores in shopping areas, are changing systematically over time as well, as are some of the social characteristics of the residents. Real incomes are increasing, and the automobile permits easy access to all parts of the city. Throughout the book we shall try to balance the fascinating uniqueness against the more useful generalization.

Canada has relatively few organizations or even individuals whose concern is primarily with urban areas, so we rely heavily on a few main sources of information. Much of the information on the external and internal pattern of cities comes directly or indirectly from the decennial census of Statistics Canada. A great wealth of material is there provided about the economic and demographic patterns in each city.

Leroy Stone's census monograph, *Urban Development in Canada,* has summarized much of this material and presents hitherto unpublished data as well. Most of the other empirical work is widely scattered in scores of professional journals, both Canadian and foreign. A wide variety of historical studies of particular cities is available but these vary enormously in depth and factual content. One must turn to the work of journalists and novelists for descriptions of the feelings of Canadians about their cities. A brief list of relevant sources follows each chapter.

BERRY, Brian J. L., *Metropolitan Area Definition: A Re-evaluation of Concept and Statistical Practice,* Working Paper 28 (Washington: U.S. Bureau of the Census, 1968). All the complications of the various urban definitions are brought forward. Equivalent discussions of Canadian practice are available in unpublished papers from Statistics Canada.

CANADIAN COUNCIL ON URBAN AND REGIONAL RESEARCH, *Urban and Regional References 1945-1966* (Ottawa: 1968 with annual supplements). This is the major bibliographic source.

JACKSON, John N., *The Canadian City: Space, Form, Quality* (Toronto: McGraw-Hill Ryerson, 1973). An extended review of the development of the physical form of cities. Examples are drawn from the Niagara area in particular.

LITHWICK, N. Harvey, *Urban Canada: Problems and Prospects,* Report to the Minister of State for Urban Affairs (Ottawa: Information Canada, 1971). An excellent review of the Canadian urban environment with particular emphasis on problem areas and potential policies.

LUCAS, Rex, *Minetown, Milltown, Railtown* (Toronto: University of Toronto Press, 1971). Examines the social structure and way of life in isolated single-industry towns.

MURDIE, Robert A. and RAY, D. Michael, "Comparisons of Canadian and American Urban Dimensions." In *Classifications of Cities: New Methods and Evolving Uses,* edited by Brian J. L. Berry (New York: John Wiley & Sons, 1971). One of a very few comparisons of Canada and the U.S., but primarily concerned with differences among cities rather than within them.

STONE, Leroy O., *Urban Development in Canada,* Statistics Canada, Census Monographs (Ottawa: Queen's Printer, 1967). The first comprehensive study of the Canadian urban pattern, focusing particularly on the demographic aspects.

WOLFORTH, John and LEIGH, Roger, *Urban Prospects* (Toronto: McClelland and Stewart, 1971). An urban textbook with a Western Canada viewpoint.

Cityscape

Vancouver *Province*

Vancouver

Calgary

National Film Board of Canada

(above) Regina

(opposite) Woodstock

Ontario Ministry of Industry and Tourism

Ontario Ministry of Industry and Tourism

(above) Toronto

(opposite) Quebec City

National Film Board of Canada

St. John's

2 The Variety of Canadian Cities

City Images

Cities are human creations and therefore tend to take on human characteristics. They are extensions of ourselves; we feel bound up in the image of the city we live in. We are participants in its past and future and affected by its successes and reversals. We take a vicarious pleasure in the activities of its prominent citizens, its sports teams, its politicians. We partake of its personality.

Moreover, we see other cities as well in terms of personality, or *image*: Hogtown Toronto, rough and raw Prince George, the ancient citadel of Quebec, Steeltown Hamilton. Citizens also are identified with their cities: the boastful Calgarian, the hard hats of Timmins, the cautious Ottawa civil servant.

A city's image seems to be a curious blend of the visual and the mythological; of the picture or landscape that leaps to mind when the city is mentioned, and of the phrase, cliché, or citizen-type that is associated with the city's character. Sudbury has a strong visual image—the slag heaps, the treeless valleys, the smoke from the smelters—which has now crystalized into a myth. If it became the garden spot of Canada the legend would remain. Some cities, though, develop strong mythological images without much apparent visual content. Most people don't know or can't remember what Moose Jaw looks like (like any other prairie town) but the name conjures up vague impressions of pioneer settlements, Dodge City and Jake and the Kid.

27

The visual picture is perhaps the more susceptible to change. Man can, and does, frequently change the visual image of his city, sometimes presenting it in some entirely new light with the addition of a single vantage point: an elevated road, a tall building, an observation tower. Calgary's Sarcee Trail gives both citizens and visitors a new image of this city, especially at night with its rows of bluish mercury vapour lamps scattered in a midnight valley. The view from the Calgary tower presents still another aspect, giving the full import of the city's rapid growth and identifying it with its foothills setting. Winnipeg, from the Trans-Canada bypass, has become a fantasy city, raising, miles away at the edge of the horizon, its floating towers through the distant prairie haze.

Or man's additions may change the city itself: Toronto's banks with their competing towers, black and white, twice as high as any of the surrounding pointed towers; Regina transformed in a few years from that quiet, green, government town to something out of Texas with its entrance highway lined with motels, gas stations, restaurants, garish signs, and construction; and, superimposed on the vision of Montreal's silvery church on the mountain, the freshly tinselled isles in the St. Lawrence.

The mythological image grows more slowly and is more difficult to modify. "Toronto the Good", "the Queen City" and "Hogtown" have emerged from countless city by-laws, political statements and censorious or jealous newspaper editorials. The city's image, which still lingers on, was one of dirt and noise, of humourless pride and prudery. Yet now, by big city standards, Toronto is clean, functional, and lively. It is still obsessed with money and pride, but the money is easier to come by—in the manner of the entrepreneur rather than the labourer—and the pride is the pride-of-place that suburban homeowners exude. In the last few years the city and the province have spent a great deal of money fixing up their lot, adding architectural extravaganzas like the City Hall, Ontario

Place, the Science Centre, and a new zoo. These very visible and widely advertised showplaces are slowly creating a new city image which is an updated suburban version of Toronto the Good, the city that's "fun" for the whole family.

The mythological and the visual may be highly related. Victoria has crowded all its symbols into one tight square— the Empress Hotel and its carefully maintained gardens face the economic symbols of the small retired harbour and the Parliament Buildings. All these features clustered together provide a post-card synthesis that the dullest observer can comprehend.

Cities being human creations, there seems to be a need to create images for them, to create unique, idiosyncratic personalities for our towns. Increasingly the communications media reinforce the slightest hint of an image, seizing some variation, amplifying or distorting it, building a permanent feature of the city. They are aided by the other city image-makers—the souvenir sellers with their stampede hats, the politicians, the Chambers of Commerce who brag about the coldest place in Canada, or support the creation of Stratford festivals.

Creating a strong image makes good business sense. The Gold Rush image of Dawson City, or the English garden quality of Victoria are carefully supported and preserved by the local businessmen. But beyond this, the citizen himself seems to have a need for this kind of city character, so much so that he finds a virtue in even the ugly or uncomfortable, like Hamilton's Steel-Mill toughness—"eat 'em raw"—or Edmonton's record twenty-one days below zero, which resulted in souvenir certificates issued to the survivors.

It is these living aspects of a city's image that writers or journalists capture so well: Mordecai Richler's Jewish Montreal, Purdy's Toronto, Roger Lemelin's Quebec City. It is the humanizing of the city that produces, and is produced by, doggerel—"Toronto squats, detested, from Vancouver to Saint John"—or novels, or features in Maclean's Magazine.

Behind the Image: Four Factors

But the urbanologist's problem is different. He is concerned, not so much with differentiating cities, as seeing similarities among them. He wants to be able to make general statements about classes or groups of cities. To do this he must get behind the image and find out which basic factors produce, in combination, the variety of Canadian city images.

Although there are vast differences between the images of Flin Flon and Winnipeg, or Quebec City and Waterloo, it may take only a few variables to describe or account for them. The four variables of size, age, setting and ethnic background will show the uniqueness of each Canadian city. The variations emerge from the many different combinations of the variables. Toronto, Montreal and Vancouver are all large, but the Montreal ethnic background is different, and Toronto and Vancouver have very different settings.

These particular four factors are the most important for distinguishing the images of Canadian cities. An infinite number of others might be applied. One could sort Canadian cities with respect to gourmet restaurants, male-female ratios, educational facilities, number of discothèques. But for getting at the basic elements of the different images that Canadian cities project, these four seem most suitable. They reflect this country's particular history, economy, topography and people.

Again, a different set of factors might well be used for another country. Age is not a factor, for example, in a country whose cities were all settled a thousand years ago. Ethnic background would not be particularly useful in a great number of racially homogeneous countries. Setting would not sort out Switzerland's towns, all of which are surrounded by mountains. And size doesn't produce enough of a distinction in countries as large as the United States, where even the larger size groupings have a number of entries.

Size

The distribution of different urban population sizes in Canada illustrates very simply two important themes: the range of variation among cities, and the overall regularities which emerge when all cities are examined together. Figure 2.1 places each urban area along the single scale of population size so that the enormity of the differences becomes apparent. Montreal is 250 times as large as Matane; Vancouver's population is equivalent to only one-third of Montreal's. Sheer difference in scale accounts for much of the other visual and social variation we observe.

2.1 City Size Distribution

Data obtained from Statistics Canada, *Census of Canada, 1971.*

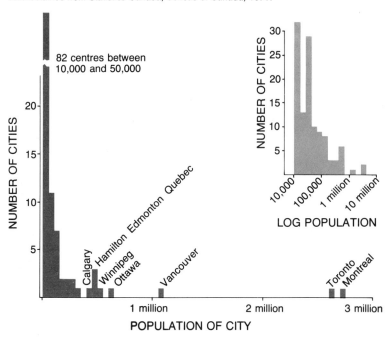

The inset diagram depicts the systematic decrease in the number of cities as the size of the city increases. The consistent step-like variation in the graph, found in many other countries as well as Canada, has a mathematical regularity which has intrigued social scientists for years. Why shouldn't all cities in a nation be the same size? Why not only two or three sizes, or more big ones than small ones, or a regular distribution about some average or optimum value? But no, the pattern is always the same. Using constant intervals on a logarithmic scale, the number of cities in any given size category will be about half as many as the number in the category containing the next smaller size of cities, and about twice as many as are contained in the category for the next larger size of cities.

Size is an important distinguishing characteristic, not because the actual number of people makes each city distinctive, but because of the qualitative changes which occur as a city gets bigger. Big cities are not just bigger versions of smaller ones, but different things.

As a city grows, noticeable changes take place. The single-activity economy and the homogeneous population give way to internal diversity and complexity. Large size implies a long, continuous growth rate requiring a diversified economy, able to respond positively to different economic environments. Larger cities provide in themselves a market for manufacturing, administration, and retail and service activities. The diversity of jobs, of stores, of recreation is an important attraction in larger cities like Toronto and Montreal. By comparison, a place like Lachute will have only three or four factories, and mining towns like Flin Flon or Trail rise and fall with the world market in zinc or gold.

As cities increase in size wider ranges of income, ethnic origin, and economic activity emerge. Each part of the original land use structure—main street, the residential area, and the economic activity which supports the town—splits up and becomes more widely separated in location and role. Suburban shopping areas develop; a new factory opens on the outskirts; and residential areas become identifiably old or new, upper income or lower. The social structure becomes more complex; a second high school is built so that you no longer know everyone in your own age group; only the old-timers or the most active citizens are personally acquainted with the civic leaders.

The continuous growth implies immigration from the full variety of Canadian sources: the Tory Loyalists or the early French settlers, the middle Europeans of the early twentieth century, and the more recent southern Europeans. The larger the city, the more diverse its population, and the more it continues to attract new immigrant groups. Montreal, Toronto, Vancouver and Winnipeg include virtually every Canadian ethnic group. Smaller places like Stratford or Joliette tend to be more homogeneous. The large city also generates the full range of architectural styles, since growth has taken place in every time period. In all these respects, big cities like Toronto and Montreal, despite apparently different cultures, are more alike than small and large cities of the same culture, such as Sept Iles and Quebec City. The larger cities share a common cosmopolitanism.

But though they grow more alike in some ways, the large cities are also more able to shape their own images and foster local traditions. They can support activities which distinguish them from others: Stanley Park, the Toronto City Hall, and Expo are single developments beyond the capacity of smaller cities. The cosmopolitanism develops distinctive local areas of specialization such as Toronto's Italian section, or Vancouver's Chinatown. The Olympic Games, a major league ball team, international conventions: these are the achievements which reassure the citizenry of the large cities.

Our definition of a city covers a range of 10,000 to 2,700,000 persons. At the smaller end of this scale are places like Amherst, Nova Scotia, and Cobourg, Ontario, barely more than towns, but with distinct functions. Towns of this size are dominated by one or two economic activities; the source of revenue is always apparent. Each town tends to be fairly homogeneous socially, with the same ethnic background and a limited range of social class. The mill town of Quebec will have a large working-class French-Canadian population; the Ontario market town is essentially a lower middle-class entrepreneurial group. Most people will act alike, vote alike, believe in the same things. They have to get along together because there are fewer alternatives than in a large city.

By the time metropolitan status is reached—seventy-five to a hundred thousand—the character and general physical outline of the city are firmly established. Land use patterns, rich areas, poor areas, the dominant economy, and the predominant ethnic groups have been fixed. The city has come into firm, though complex, focus. Representatives of different social classes exist and become formally recognized. Country clubs, union halls, churches of different kinds, pawn shops and boutiques emerge.

Beyond this stage the complexities multiply, recognizing the infinite possibilities of variation in each social group. Neighbourhoods are differentiated until there is an area to suit everyone. At the same time the massive large-scale developments—1,000-unit apartment complexes, new suburban towns, and industrial parks—are built, altering the face of the whole city. Increasing city size is expressed in these two opposite directions: specialization and diversity on one hand, and the homogeneity of huge enterprises on the other.

Age

The age of Canadian cities is another differentiating factor producing a different sort-out of cities. In Canada, the older cities are not necessarily the largest; in fact, the converse

34

is more likely to be true, because of the relatively slow growth of the older cities of the Maritimes. Saint John, which became a city in 1792, has long since been passed by Edmonton which was chartered in 1904.

The downtown business district or the port are most likely to show the visual marks of age: narrow, even crooked streets, and old, brick, three-story warehouses and store fronts. In the Maritimes, incredibly weathered wooden buildings continue to survive because of the lack of incentive to replace them.

However, the distinguishing characteristics of age may be obscured in very large old cities because of their continued growth and prosperity, which lead to major redevelopment of older parts of the city. Toronto retains little trace of the early nineteenth-century settlement, and the late nineteenth-century buildings are fast disappearing, torn down for parking lots, office buildings, apartments. In rapidly growing metropolitan areas a site in the city centre may be rebuilt three or four times in the course of a century. It is in the smaller old cities whose size has tended to change less rapidly in recent years, that the marks of age are most visible, still part of the city's image.

Nevertheless, the period in which a settlement first grows to city size does leave important effects, even in the continuously growing city. The early concentration of stores and jobs in the town centre affects the developing residential patterns of the city. Older cities have much higher population densities near the city centre. More recent cities begin with more decentralized employment and service activities, so that high central densities never develop. The critical point in time is the introduction of the automobile. Those cities laid out after World War I have more spacious arterial streets and are much more spread out than cities which relied on the pedestrian or even the trolley car. The relics of early urban growth may also include blocks of graceful residences, as in Kingston or Fredericton; or, on the darker side, the appalling slum conditions of

Montreal where numbers of early nineteenth-century buildings cling to life, becoming yearly more dilapidated.

The character of some older cities is more interestingly, or more aesthetically, shown by institutions or buildings dating from the very early settlement: the open farmers' markets in Kitchener and Ottawa; the distinctive, curving main street of St. Catharines; the towering, domed, Roman Catholic church dominating the hill around which Guelph has grown.

Older cities also possess the historical and institutional base on which to build elaborate and traditional social structures, with the élite restricted to the descendants of early merchants. Traditional "society" institutions and events—men's clubs, balls, hunts, garden parties, private schools—manifest the Establishment in London or Quebec City or St. John's. Although any relatively wealthy, Anglo-Saxon newcomer can be quickly accepted in London, he must for his part surrender to the traditions and values of the city, join the right clubs, and accept the right invitations. In this way the traditional structure is maintained and this aspect of the city remains unchanged.

At the other end of the scale from "ancient" is "instant", the urban centres which have undergone much of their growth within the past twenty years: Calgary, Edmonton, Oshawa, Brampton. These cities appear to be composed entirely of suburbs and shopping plazas and wide arterial streets which a pedestrian crosses at his own risk. Downtown is relatively undistinguished, and the city gives an overall impression of sprawl and decentralization. Workers commute across the city to widely dispersed jobs. Any traces of early buildings or street plans are rapidly being erased by new massive office towers or high-rise apartments.

The social patterns as well as the visual impressions differ in the late-blooming cities. The old establishment is overwhelmed by the newcomers. Of the present residents seventy to eighty per cent have moved into the city from somewhere else, creating a common bond of transiency, like freshmen in college or new recruits in the army. People remark on how friendly the city is, or how easy it is to meet people. With no established social patterns, no kinship ties, everyone is a newcomer and a potential ally.

The population age pattern of these cities is dominated by the highly mobile age groups, 20 to 35, and their hordes of small children. Because of the preoccupation with child-bearing and the need to pay off the mortgage, social life revolves around home and family. Churches and service clubs will be more successful than strip-joints or gay bars. The swingers will find such cities barren places. People used to a variety of artistic enterprises will mutter bitterly about a "wasteland". But such lacks reflect the demographic structure rather than the political or ethnic environment. If the theatres, restaurants and cafés of Montreal had to depend on suburbs like Beaconsfield or Roxboro for support, Rue Ste. Catherine would soon resemble Calgary's 8th Avenue.

The character of the civic leadership—political, economic and social—also depends on when the city achieves its major growth. A place which has stopped growing will be run by old-timers: a few merchants nursing their decaying businesses out of gloomy back rooms with tin-plate ceilings; Senator X, the defeated politician, too senile even for a judgeship; perhaps a crusty third-generation mill owner, or an equally crusty old union-leader who learned his tactics before the First World War. Their public statements, their priorities for public expenditure—keep the mill rate down!—their reactions to innovation, all affect the town's image of itself and the image projected to visitors.

At the other extreme, the leaders of the new suburban communities are a brisk, thirtyish, white-shirt-sleeves kind of people, young engineers or business administration graduates. Their native intelligence is probably no higher; they are not innately more concerned with improving the quality of urban life, but they speak the jargon of the late twentieth century, of growth and development, planning and investment, and they have an optimism for all kinds of projects which in turn shapes the attitudes of the citizens.

Setting

A powerful component of the visual image of a Canadian city is its physical setting. Vancouver, Montreal and Quebec City are instantly recognizable from the terrain, but coming into Calgary or Winnipeg from the air presents an equally striking picture. Ottawa, Victoria, Halifax: each of them occupies a unique topographical site which constitutes an important urban symbol.

Most Canadian cities have a distinctive site. Many of them are lake or ocean ports or on major rivers, so that the site characteristics are linked to the economy and history of the place. Interaction and land use patterns are determined in part by the distribution of slope and of water. This is what differentiates Niagara Falls from Brantford, and Saint John (river mouth, N.B.) from St. John's, (sea-port, Nfld.).

Climate varies more gradually over space, but to a sufficient degree to give cities of different regions part of their flavour. The memorable rainy season of Vancouver, the inspiring cold of January in Winnipeg, the steamy July of Windsor and Ottawa are treasured and exaggerated by the local citizens, and ultimately become part of the myth of each city.

The physical setting, both terrain and climate, links the city, its past, and its surrounding region. The relative consistency of the setting over time permits the comparison of the early smaller city with the later larger one. The old lithographs of Bytown are still easily recognizable, and on them we can superimpose the Ottawa of today. The setting is the major reminder that an earlier Canada was tied to the land, that cities are still representative of the great physical regions of the country. The mountains remind a Vancouverite that he lives in God's country; the fogs of Halifax suggest the sea and its importance for the town. From practically anywhere in Calgary you can see the bare foothills, the peaks of the Rockies, the incredible breadth of sky, and get an instant reinforcement of place. By contrast, the lush greenness of trees of the cities in Southern Ontario creates an atmosphere of comfort and fertility.

Ethnic Background

The origins of a Canadian city's inhabitants may also contribute to its image. Victoria has been immortalized by the Norris cartoons as the home of retired British military men and rich dowager ladies. Vancouver has a cosmopolitan, distinctly oriental air, while Calgary reflects the Midwestern American origins of many of its people.

Figure 2.2 gives some idea of the variations in ethnic origin in Canadian cities. Several cities are predominantly of British descent—the traditional cities of Saint John, Victoria, Halifax and London—and many cities have a very high concentration of French ancestry, over ninety per cent in most cases. Only Montreal of the Quebec cities has a significant concentration of peoples of non-British, non-French origin. Most of the recent immigrants from Europe have opted for English-speaking areas.

A few cities—Ottawa, Sudbury and Windsor—are bicultural in French and English; but a number of western cities have large proportions of Ukrainians, Scandinavians, Polish, Germans and Dutch. Thunder Bay is the best Ontario example of this kind of ethnic mixture. The population of every

2.2 Ethnic Diversity

Data obtained from Statistics Canada, *Census of Canada, 1971.*

This chart indicates the proportion of a city's population composed of each of three different ethnic origins. The closer a city is to a point of the triangle, the more homogeneous is its ethnic origin.

Note the extreme homogeneity of most Quebec cities, and the spectrum of British and other origins in the remainder of the country.

▲ Census metropolitan areas

● Other urban areas >40,000

100% BRITISH DESCENT

THE LOYALIST TOWNS

ONTARIO INDUSTRIAL CITIES AND WESTERN CITIES

100% OTHER ETHNIC ORIGINS (German, Italian, Ukrainian)

100% FRENCH DESCENT

QUEBEC

● St. John's
● Peterborough
▲ Saint John
● Kingston
▲ Halifax
● Sydney
● Victoria
▲ London
● Brantford
● Sarnia
● Oshawa
● Guelph
▲ Hamilton
● North Bay
▲ Moncton
▲ Toronto
▲ Vancouver
▲ Kamloops
● St. Catharines
▲ Calgary
● Prince George
▲ Windsor
▲ Kitchener
● Lethbridge
▲ Sault Ste. Marie
● Saskatoon
● Edmonton
● Regina
▲ Winnipeg
● Cornwall
▲ Ottawa
● Thunder Bay
▲ Sudbury
● Timmins
▲ Montreal
▲ Sherbrooke
▲ St. Jean
● Chicoutimi
● Quebec
▲ Shawinigan
● Drummondville
▲ Trois Rivières

Canadian city is at least 40 per cent French or British in descent, and it is this two-nation cultural bifurcation that sorts Canadian cities immediately into two main groups.

Not a large proportion of an ethnic group is required to put its imprint on a city's image. The differences from city to city are really not that great, as we have seen, but a group arriving at the critical growth period of a city, or one in control of its physical and institutional development, can have an extremely powerful and lasting influence. Fredericton and Kingston still show the conservative effects of the British Protestant Loyalist stock which settled them over 150 years ago. Even the casual observer quickly notes the Germanic names of retail stores as he enters Kitchener-Waterloo, or the abundance of thistle and tartan symbols in Brockville.

The first impressions of ethnic background come from superficial visual symbols: the names on store fronts, the Chamber of Commerce literature. But essentially the image is a people thing, the whole complex of subtle accents and customs which reflect a previous or different background: the midwestern accents in Calgary, the little girls with gold earrings in the Italian sections of Hamilton and Sudbury, the poise and dress, the flair, of the girls in Quebec City.

When two groups challenge each other for dominance, the clash or contrast makes the ethnic components of a city particularly visible. In the cities of the Eastern Townships—Sherbrooke, Granby and Magog—the English names of streets, and the old buildings so similar to those of many parts of Ontario, counterpoint the completely French-speaking culture. In Toronto the black-clad Italian grandmothers sit calmly in front of mock-gothic Victorian row-houses.

The Diversity of Canadian Cities

Canadian cities have strong distinctive images. They tend to maintain these idiosyncratic flavours despite their dependence on the national economy and the closeness of their links with other cities. The names Fredericton, Moose Jaw, Ottawa, produce a reaction in people, conjure up a cliché. Why?

In part this diversity, this apparent uniqueness, is due to the small number of Canadian cities, compared to the huge continental land mass they share. When there are only 22 metropolitan areas, and 116 cities over 10,000, our four simple variables sort them out readily. The small number also helps to make Canadians remarkably familiar with their urban areas. Most of us, if we have not visited the major cities ourselves, have friends or relatives in Montreal, Ottawa, Toronto, Winnipeg, Calgary or Vancouver. Anyone who has driven cross-country has passed through most of them.

But partly, also, the strong images of Canadian cities are a result of the great contrasts, the wide swings between the extremes of each dimensional scale. Canada has only three very large cities, Toronto, Montreal, and Vancouver; consequently, all the way down the steps of the size pyramid, the number of cities in each category is smaller. On the age dimension, Canada's very long history of continuous city-making, which extends from 1608 right up to the creation of Thompson in 1967, gives a full range of possibilities, and produces strong contrasts between St. John's and Bramalea. The vast size of the country also produces a strong contrast between extremes of setting and climate. And the presence of two major language groups, together with the fact that immigration is a continuing part of Canada's growth pattern, produces greater than usual extremes of ethnic differentiation.

And so the French-Canadian mill town of Drummondville, and the WASP Ontario agricultural service centre of

2.3 Cosmopolitan Cities

*This graph indicates how cosmopolitan a city is for its size, at
least by one measure. The solid red portion indicates the proportion of a city's inhabitants born outside Canada; the striped red
portion, those people born in a different province; the striped
black portion, those born in the same province.*

Data obtained from Statistics Canada, *Census of Canada, 1971.*

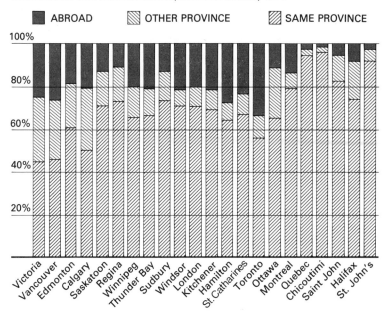

Stratford, and the new mining and lumbering boom town of
Prince George in northern British Columbia, can coexist very
vividly in a single country, and produce strikingly different
images.

The similarities which do exist among Canadian cities are
primarily regional. In a very general way relationships among
the differentiating characteristics can be found, so that a rapidly
growing city, for instance, will probably be located in the West,
and will have a greater proportion of people with a continental
European background. Figure 2.3, measuring the cosmopolitanism of Canadian cities by the proportion of the popula-

tion born outside the province, demonstrates the regional variation. Note the gradual increase in this proportion as one moves westward, reflecting the general movement of the Canadian population from East to West.

Aside from Quebec, which contains some of the oldest and newest urban areas in Canada, and is distinguished by its French-speaking Roman Catholic populace, the variations along the dimensions are regular from East to West, and are linked with the period of settlement. The Maritimes contain the older, slow-growing, lower-income towns, composed almost entirely of British stock. The cities of the West Coast and Alberta are fast-growing and based on the service and professional activities of the last few decades. They have a more diverse ethnic mix. Ontario lies between these extremes, its cities distinguished from those of the East and West only for their manufacturing specialization.

HABITAT, "The Centennial Issue," X, Numbers 3-6 (1967). Thirty-four prominent Canadians take a look at their home towns. The variations in cities and their self-images are strongly emphasized.

LYNCH, Kevin, *The Image of the City* (Cambridge, Mass.: Harvard University Press, 1960). The classic and readable investigation of how people view and understand their city.

RASHLEIGH, Edward T., "Observations on Canadian Cities, 1960-61," *Plan Canada* III (September, 1962) pp. 60-77. Some perceptive comments by an outsider.

RAY, D. Michael, *Dimensions of Canadian Regionalism,* Geographical Paper No. 49 (Ottawa: Information Canada, 1972). A rather technical evaluation of the differences between city and regions—this is the urbanologist's approach.

3 The Origins of Urban Canada

The Sequence of Urban Development

Urban Canada began with the first explorers, the first traders. These were urban people engaged in urban activities, in command of or in contact with large groups of people, engaged in buying and selling, themselves the products of London and Paris life. The rural settlers and farmers came much later in Canada's history.

The study of the evolution of the first ports and trading posts, and later of the gradual diffusion of settlement through the spread of service centres, from East to West and inland from the major waterways, reveals the origin of regional and economic differences between cities. It also helps explain some of the more anomalous urban images. The good Orange Toronto and Cowtown Calgary were roles that were very real for a long time. Only in the last two decades has extensive growth irrevocably altered them.

Economically, Canada's long dependence on "staple" products, the raw materials so susceptible to swings in world markets, has made her cities prone to rapid change, and kept her continuously in the process of founding them. Mining or lumbering towns bloom overnight, even today, only to fade away, or change roles completely. Successful Canadian towns are a product of their economic roles, and those functions developed at certain key points in their histories. The process of urban development explains many of the similarities and differences of Canadian cities.

45

The development of the present urban Canada as a whole can be traced in three stages. Long before towns emerged, today's urban pattern was foreshadowed by an elaborate system of forts, missions, and trading posts. The critical locations and the important sites were identified, although actual urban development did not occur until agricultural settlement took place in the regions, creating a need for service centres to supply necessities and markets. Finally, the agricultural towns were transformed according to the needs of the national economy, and specialization in industry or government, transportation or defense, took place.

Not all cities went through these phases, of course. Many of the fur trade posts never achieved urban status. Later on, the settlement stage demanded many more centres than the outposts could provide, and many Canadian cities were founded at that stage. Some of these places were later to evolve into industrial towns or administrative centres. Canada continues to create specialized places directly from the wilderness, such as the resource towns along the northern frontier. As a general model, however, relevant for such diverse places as Quebec, Toronto, Vancouver and Saint John, the sequence of outpost, service centre, and specialized place is useful.

We must also keep in mind that urbanization in the broad sense, the increase in the proportion of persons living in cities, has taken place throughout Canadian history. In every decade the growth of urban places has been more rapid than the over-all national growth; and in each part of the country the initial spread of agricultural settlement has been followed by a continuous retreat to the cities.

Given this sequence of development—outpost, rural settlement and urban development, and specialization—we can see that the usual rural-to-urban model doesn't quite fit. Outposts generally drew people together into intensely interacting groups, often composed of a cosmopolitan and heterogeneous population. These are urban characteristics. But the size of these outposts was small and so the number of roles to be played was limited—a rural pattern. The early outposts, then, were neither urban nor rural, but a composite of both.

Then came the agricultural settlement, and with it the network of urban service centres needed to service the outlying farms. But these towns, while large in size, leaned toward rural values for two reasons. First, they were dependent on rural customers; and second, homogeneity, rather than heterogeneity, was stressed in these service towns, which consisted largely of buyers and sellers, rather than specialized industrial workers in different fields. The resulting inclination toward rural values is still to be seen in the cities and towns of Canada's West today.

Only with the development of specialized economic functions in cities, does a completely urban culture come into being. This is accompanied by still greater increases in the size of cities. And when this happens, once again urban life styles and values tend to dominate, not only the urban centres, but the whole country. The urban shop-keepers now influence the rural customers who are no longer catered to as a majority, but whose products are relegated to the back of the store, as befits a minority.

Urban Outposts

Long before the spread of settlement, key sites throughout the country were staked out by the various agents of imperialism. Generals, fur traders, and missionaries built forts, trading posts and churches to protect their interests. The locations were chosen by much the same criteria which make a city significant today: access to the surrounding region, or critical connections along a transportation route. It is unlikely that these

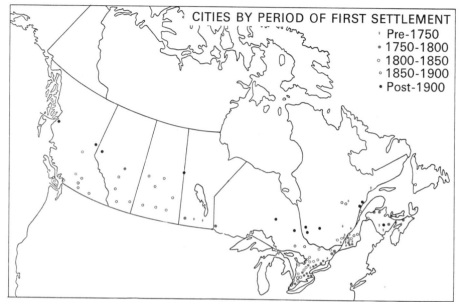

CITIES BY PERIOD OF FIRST SETTLEMENT
' Pre-1750
• 1750-1800
∘ 1800-1850
∘ 1850-1900
• Post-1900

3.1 **The Spread of Urban Places**

entrepreneurs foresaw the long-run implications of their decisions, but the rules for locating an efficient mission or a prosperous fur house are much the same as for placing a wholesale dry goods business. Such places became natural settlement centres as well, attracting to an area newcomers who wanted protection, access to other human beings, supplies and markets—all the forms of moral and economic support required for pioneering.

Figure 3.1 identifies the date of first settlement of present-day cities, ignoring the much greater number of potential cities which were founded with high hopes but never made it. The gradual extension of settlement from the Atlantic to the Pacific is apparent, although distorted considerably by

48

the pattern of inland waterways. Settlement followed the St. Lawrence, the Atlantic Coast, the Great Lakes, the prairie rivers —the Assiniboine and the Saskatchewan—and then the Pacific. The time lag in settlement increases rapidly as one goes inland from the waterways. The fur traders built their first fort on Thunder Bay before 1700; Portage la Prairie (1738), Winnipeg (1738), even Edmonton (1795), were located before inland Ontario was settled.

The map also ignores the pre-European settlements which were often of considerable size. The sites of Quebec and Montreal were each occupied by a series of Indian villages. Hochelaga, now Montreal, is described by Cartier as having over fifty long houses, each containing several families. The megalopolis of the Huron Indians consisted of several shifting settlements between Georgian Bay and Lake Simcoe, and contained a population of about 16,000 in the early 17th century.

The first permanent recorded European settlement at any of our urban places was Quebec, founded in 1608 by Champlain, although there was a premature settlement at the site some seventy years before. Another possible contender for first settlement is the ancient port of St. John's, Newfoundland. Its origin is obscure, but fishermen from the western shores of Europe fished the Grand Banks for a hundred years before the founding of Quebec.

Quebec and Montreal set the Canadian settlement pattern for the next hundred and fifty years. A fortified town, protected by a military garrison, maintained the rights of France and the Church in the New World, guarded access to the fur trade, and protected a cluster of nearby farms. Forts and trading posts were established along the Atlantic coast to maintain the Acadian settlements around present-day cities such as Charlottetown (Port Lajoie, 1720) and Saint John (Fort LaTour, 1631).

Within Quebec a tightly knit urban system emerged, linked by the navigable rivers. All along the St. Lawrence, the

49

Saguenay, the Richelieu and other rivers, forts became the foci of settlements, and most of these places moved through the stages of outpost and rural service centre to become specialized industrial towns in the twentieth century. A common history, economic base, physical setting and ethnicity link Sorel, St. Jean, Chambly and others.

The cities of Quebec and Montreal maintained their pre-eminence against all comers, however, with Quebec as the political, military and religious centre and Montreal rapidly becoming the commercial centre. By 1685 the former had a population of 1100 but Montreal had overtaken it with a population of 1205. Undoubtedly the city fathers of the respective places passed angry notes back and forth to France about the favouritism shown to their rival.

Rural Canada

Gradually, in each region agricultural settlements spread out over the land and became the predominant economic activity. Some of the posts and forts were developed to serve the rural economy, and where no previous sites were available new centres and towns sprang up. The major role of the city was to serve the surrounding population, and it was not until this stage of economic development that cities as we know them (in terms of size) became a viable proposition.

In Eastern Canada the changeover happened relatively quickly. The British took over Quebec in 1763; the American Revolution took place in 1776-1781, followed by the War of 1812-14. Each of these events provided impetus for creating permanent settlements in Canada. In 1763 French-Canadian settlement in Quebec was still small (less than 70,000) and largely confined to the navigable river system, but the British superimposed on this limited pattern a massive settlement of

British soldiers, American Tories, and emigrants from the British Isles. Later, settlers from Germany and the United States were to follow them, and by 1850 settlement was fairly complete in the Maritimes, Ontario and Quebec.

In the process a new urban system was created with cities founded for different reasons, requiring different locations and with differing economic roles. Swords turned to plowshares; soldiers became settlers and administrators; strategic sites became less important than good agricultural land. The more fortunate of the outposts found themselves relevant to the new economic patterns and became major commercial centres: Toronto (founded 1690), Kingston (1673) and Saint John (1631), for instance. But many more centres were required inland from the major waterways in the agricultural areas. Peterborough and Drummondville are typical of this particular settlement wave. Cities of this era have a less romantic and cosmopolitan background. Their role is more that of the agricultural service centre, with a little industry on the side.

Figure 3.1 shows the new towns founded in inland Ontario and Quebec during this period. Peterborough, Bytown (to become Ottawa), Belleville, Hamilton, St. Jerome, Drummondville, Granby first emerged to serve the local agricultural region. Most of them later attracted specialized economic activities.

The growth of these service centres was not automatic. Small towns like Niagara-on-the-Lake, Morrisburg and Richmond were once larger than London, Kitchener or Chicoutimi, but could not maintain their early pace. Other centres with better locations reduced the trade areas of the less fortunate towns, and industrial or government activities never arrived to rescue them. The twenty-five largest urban areas designated in Figure 3.4 are the present leaders in a continuing struggle for survival. A few ambitious homes and elaborate town plans are all that remain of the hopes and capital invested in hundreds upon hundreds of villages and towns that once challenged Montreal or Winnipeg.

In Eastern Canada the successful urban settlement could emerge in a variety of ways. Initially a location on a water route was important. Settlers disembarked from the river and lake boats which had carried them inland, and in the local centre purchased and registered their property. Settlement required investment in livestock, tools, seed, and food, and soon the original trading post was in competition with half a dozen general merchants and taverns. Property dealings brought lawyers and administrators. Soldiers, bureaucrats, doctors, stevedores, carpenters, blacksmiths followed.

In addition, the rapid population growth in the areas under settlement required great investment in government facilities. Ports, roads, courthouses, and garrisons were needed in order to administer and control the newly settled land. Arbitrary decisions by distant governments about the location of these activities determined the fate of many potential cities. Very early in the settlement process, Fredericton, London, and Sherbrooke were designated as administrative centres and became the foci of settlement within their regions, providing county seats, garrisons and transportation terminals.

And, ultimately, water power became an asset, for timber to be sawed and grain to be ground. Here the up-country towns had the advantage, and this particular service activity often led to the beginnings of industrial development in the next stage.

The urban places of the West depended almost entirely on the railroad. The building of the C.P.R., linking the lakehead to Vancouver, required a whole network of service centres almost overnight. In Winnipeg or Brandon the trading post provided an obvious site, but where posts were absent or unsatisfactorily located the railways created towns at arbitrary intervals. Moose Jaw, Swift Current, Medicine Hat, Calgary were largely created as railway-serving towns, a hundred or so miles apart. Regina, with nothing to distinguish it from an infinite number of other points on the prairie, was designated to be the provincial capital of Saskatchewan. Calgary, an RCMP fort from a few years earlier, became the gateway to the main pass through the Rockies. Saskatoon, Yorkton, North Battleford, and Red Deer emerged soon after as regional trading centres. Although urbanization has continued on the prairies, the region has still not entered the third phase of urban settlement. The role of each city was determined in the first wave of agricultural settlement and very few relative shifts have occurred among the cities since that time. Again a set of cities with common backgrounds, settings and attitudes is identified. The only exception is the stimulus of the oil economy in Calgary and Edmonton, and if anything, oil appears to have amplified the conservative region-serving attitudes typical of prairie cities.

The period of rural settlement left a powerful imprint on urban Canada. The nation believed that the city depended on the farmer, that the rural economy must be protected, and that rurally-oriented politicians should dominate the provincial and federal levels of government. Rural life, agricultural markets, tariffs, and settlement policies were the pervasive concerns of novelists, journalists, and politicians.

During this period, too, the competitive nature of the urban economy became important, as cities attempted to increase their hinterland and to attract new customers and new activities. As the whole urban network became more closely integrated, a city's prosperity began to depend on its location and linkages with respect to other cities. The desperate battles for rail links and the wild canal schemes took place at this stage in the economy, and produced the "boosterism" of Chambers of Commerce which remains today.

Then, as cities grew more economically independent of the immediate region, the gap between urban and rural needs and values increased. Cities became necessary evils, not to be entrusted with political power. Their growth and prosperity were to be discouraged, and their dust, noise, pollution and vice made the good life unattainable, and virtue impossible.

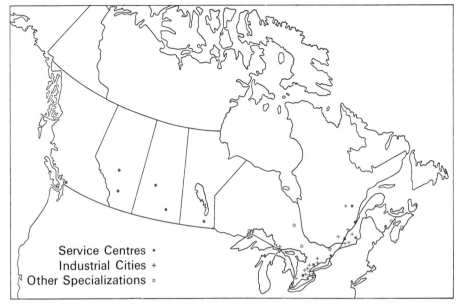

Service Centres •
Industrial Cities +
Other Specializations ○

3.2 **Economic Specialization**

The Specialized Economy

As the nation grew and life-styles became more complex, as Canada's role in the international economy changed, urban Canada developed new jobs. Factories were required; mining and pulp and paper became important continuing activities; ports and rail centres were needed, and the nation's government and defense programme had to be expanded.

These new activities, employing many of the people in urban clusters, were superimposed on the pattern of thousands of rural service centres of varying sizes. But since these activities served a national, even international economy, they were not necessarily distributed in size and space in the same way as the local service centres. Sometimes a regional centre such as London or Sherbrooke absorbed some industry and federal employment in addition to its local commercial role, but only if the original centre were located centrally with respect to the larger market. Many smaller places such as Kitchener or Chicoutimi expanded very rapidly to urban status because of their suitability for specialized economic activities.

The process of industrialization is most evident in Ontario and Quebec. By 1850 the agricultural development was pretty well complete and a full complement of service centres existed, sufficient to serve the agricultural population with stores, lawyers and bureaucrats. Within twenty or thirty years the density of rural population reached a peak and then out-migration began. The alternatives for the youngest son were to go west and homestead, or to go to the nearby cities.

During the same period the cities became linked by an efficient transportation system. An intricate net of railways existed by 1880, complementing a continuously improving network of waterways. As wider markets became available, access to the larger system became important.

Towns located on the railways soon overwhelmed their bypassed neighbours. Tremendous competition took place between neighbouring towns to lure the railway. Lake ports like Cobourg and Port Hope even built their own railways into the interior. It was during this period that the railways could demand and obtain their incredible concessions—free land, tax exemption, the best sites in the city—concessions which were to distort spatial patterns within the city for a century. But the city fathers of 1850 were perceptive enough to realize that they had no choice; without a railroad, a city could not survive.

Industrial towns emerged in a variety of locations. Any settlement was a potential factory town as long as it lay within reach of the Central Canada market. The larger service centres, with their existing labour forces, markets, and entrepreneurs, were more likely to develop industry than smaller places; but

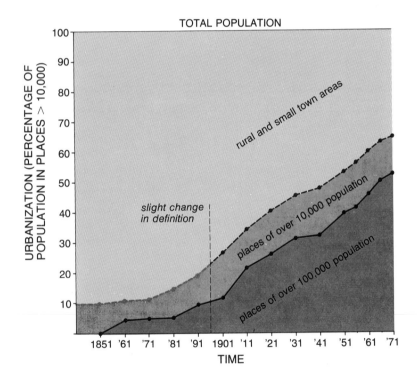

PERCENTAGE OF CANADIANS LIVING IN:

●----● places of over 10,000 population

●——● places of over 100,000 population

TOTAL POPULATION

URBANIZATION (PERCENTAGE OF POPULATION IN PLACES > 10,000)

rural and small town areas

slight change in definition

places of over 10,000 population

places of over 100,000 population

1851 '61 '71 '81 '91 1901 '11 '21 '31 '41 '51 '61 '71

TIME

3.3 **Urbanization of Canada**

Data obtained from Statistics Canada, *Census of Canada*, for various years.

the successful craftsman whose small workshop grew into a great factory could create a town almost anywhere. R. S. McLaughlin of Oshawa parlayed his carriage factory into part of General Motors and transformed a small town into an important city.

Often water power attracted a nucleus of mills, which later developed into an industrial complex. Cowansville and Granby started in this fashion. Location with respect to the transportation network helped others. Hamilton's port and strategic situation on the Great Lakes highway made it a steel centre. Windsor grew because of its proximity to Detroit-based industry, and was a natural location for activities selling to the American market. Other places, like Kitchener, Brantford, Peterborough and St. Jerome, just seemed to grow gradually into industrial centres, with a wide range of firms and activities. During this period, too, the exploitation of natural resources led to highly specialized urban places. Sudbury, Asbestos, and Thetford Mines were mining towns; Rimouski, Edmundston, and Campbellton were pulp and paper towns.

By 1914 the urban network in Central Canada was much more like today's pattern. The winners and losers in the economic competition had been identified. Areas of rapid urban growth were already apparent, and Toronto and Montreal were growing most rapidly of all.

But in the Maritimes and the Prairies, industrialization never really took place. Sydney and New Glasgow developed steel mills, based on their ample coal supply, but by and large, markets were too far away for factories to prosper. The same towns continued to fulfil the same service functions, growing slowly as the region grew. The urban patterns of these areas have long been the most stable of all, as cities maintain the same rank relative to the others.

One more economic region with its own urban typology is currently coming into existence in Canada. North of the agricultural settlements, new resource-oriented towns are emerging to

1851	1901	1941	1971	RANK BY POPULATION
MONTREAL (79.7)	Montreal (392.1)	Montreal (1193.2)	Montreal (2587.3)	1
QUEBEC (45.5)	Toronto (270.9)	Toronto (865.7)	Toronto (2465.1)	2
TORONTO (30.8)	Quebec (88.6)	Vancouver (338.3)	Vancouver (1026.9)	3
ST. JOHN'S (30.5)	OTTAWA (85.3)	Winnipeg (302.0)	Ottawa (555.0)	4
SAINT JOHN (23.7)	Hamilton (83.3)	Hamilton (224.7)	Winnipeg (540.3)	5
HALIFAX (20.7)	LONDON (51.6)	Ottawa (208.9)	Hamilton (488.9)	6
HAMILTON (17.6)	Saint John (51.2)	Quebec (196.7)	Edmonton (486.7)	7
KINGSTON (11.6)	Halifax (51.0)	Windsor (128.6)	Quebec (463.3)	8
	WINNIPEG (48.5)	EDMONTON (124.9)	Calgary (403.3)	9
	VANCOUVER (43.4)	CALGARY (111.6)	Windsor (237.6)	10
	St. John's (40.0)	Halifax (98.6)	London (235.8)	11
	KITCHENER (36.0)	London (97.2)	Kitchener (226.8)	12
	SYDNEY-GLACE BAY (35.7)	Sydney-Glace Bay (96.7)	Halifax (204.8)	13
	VICTORIA (23.5)	Kitchener (82.8)	Victoria (195.8)	14
	WINDSOR (22.4)	Victoria (81.0)	SUDBURY (145.0)	15
		Saint John (70.9)	Regina (139.5)	16
		St. John's (60.9)	SASKATOON (126.4)	17
		REGINA (58.8)	ST. CATHARINES (124.8)	18
		THUNDER BAY (56.3)	OSHAWA (119.4)	19
		TROIS RIVIERES (56.3)	St. John's (112.4)	20
			CHICOUTIMI-JONQUIERE (109.1)	21
			Thunder Bay (108.4)	22
			Sydney-Glace Bay (106.0)	23
			Saint John (102.1)	24
			Trois Rivières (96.9)	25
	Kingston (19.8) (rank 16)	Kingston (34.8) (rank 30)	Kingston (76.8) (rank 28)	

3.4 Population Stability of the Canadian Urban System
Each time a new city is introduced to the chart, it appears in
capital letters. Note the difference in the growth rates of
Quebec and Saint John. Data obtained from Statistics Canada,
Census of Canada, for various years, using the 1961 spatial definition
of a census metropolitan area.

serve miners and pulp and paper workers, and to exploit hydro power. Nine of our present list of 116 cities over 10,000 were founded after 1914, and several more recently created towns will achieve city status within the next few years. Baie Comeau, Thompson, Kapuskasing, Rouyn, Noranda and Val d'Or are now cities, but were unheard of at the beginning of the century. Each grew to serve a specific resource development project.

About 20 per cent of Canadians now live in "single-industry" towns. Life in these places is a complex mixture of urban intensity and rural routine, with the social structure determined by the plant and its needs. These towns used to have a special flavour: tough, grubby, masculine towns; lots of single men, and hard drinking; isolated in god-awful places wherever the mine-head or mill happened to be. Recently, the goal has been to build planned communities, designed to grow to a specific size, and in proper relation to the mine or mill. The idea is to encourage families to come at an early stage and provide a docile working force.

The trouble with these cities is the basic instability of such specialized economic activity. Elliott Lake, the uranium town north of Sudbury, is the classic example of the on-again off-again nature of this kind of urban economy. The uranium market depends on government policy, decided in Ottawa and Washington. Anticipating prosperity, the Ontario government invested millions of dollars to create a suburban environment for the workers, only to be left with a ghost town a few years later.

The development of the specialized economy of urban Canada sharpened once again the rift between rural and urban. It gave cities new independence, new roles, and attracted new people whose values were not the same as those of the farmers nearby. Immigrants from Eastern and Southern Europe, trade-unionists and intellectuals became prominent in cities. Urban Canada became less dependent on and less conscious of the regional environment, and more irked by rural attitudes in the senior levels of government.

Metropolitanization

As urban Canada evolves and becomes more independent of the non-urban areas, new phenomena are emerging. The great metropolitan centres, Montreal, Toronto and Vancouver, now dominate a wide area surrounding their cores, and produce rapid urban growth in small centres for miles around. Improved accessibility through the construction of high-speed expressways has caused one-time sleepy service centres like Brampton, or St. Jean, to explode into growth.

As cities grow to metropolitan size they become less specialized economically, and more like one another. A greater proportion of their economy is devoted to serving the needs of the city and the nearby area. These needs, of course, grow with the growth of the city, and at a certain size level, they generate administrative and manufacturing enterprises as well as stores. The city's own market is sufficient to support various small industries and specialized public services.

At this size level—in Canada, perhaps about 500,000 persons—the growth impetus becomes self-sustaining. The local market creates a great deal of demand, attracting establishments which can then, given their solid local base, afford to grow to a point where they sell to a national or international market. High wages and highly skilled labour lead to innovation and improvement. Ideas lead to new firms and more efficient methods of production.

Three Canadian centres appear to have reached this self-sustaining plateau: Montreal, Toronto and Vancouver. These centres are characterized by a diverse economy, a complex social structure, and continued growth. It means that they will share in all the future growth of the national economy, and presumably play a larger and larger part within the nation. They are more able to control their own fortunes, maintain their images and use their political power.

60

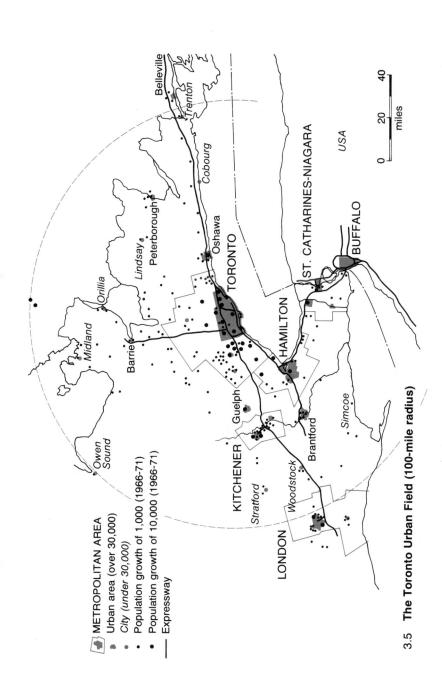

METROPOLITAN AREA
Urban area (over 30,000)
City (under 30,000)
• Population growth of 1,000 (1966-71)
● Population growth of 10,000 (1966-71)
— Expressway

3.5 **The Toronto Urban Field (100-mile radius)**

Calgary, Edmonton, Winnipeg and Ottawa may be ready to move into this category. Ottawa's growth seems inevitable unless the country goes broke or splits up. There only remains to be seen whether that city's economy will diversify. The western metropolises, however, with their various regional economic bases, are still somewhat too susceptible to world markets and the international economy.

The major aim of regional economic assistance is to create these kinds of urban growth points, to build self-sufficient cities in slow-growth regions which will continue to grow by themselves and ultimately support the regional economy. If St. John's, Halifax and Saint John can maintain a consistent rate of growth and develop a diversified economy, Canada will have gone a long way toward solving regional disparities.

The central city of each metropolitan area embraces a host of smaller centres nearby which have grown under its influence, until finally a complex multi-centred metropolitan region emerges. The influence of the metropolis extends up to a hundred miles in each direction, changing the economy in a variety of ways. The agriculture is intensified because of the market in dairy products and fruits and vegetables, and the pressures of land speculators. Recreation developments to serve the city surround every brook, every ridge, every irregularity in the terrain within a day's travel. The growth of towns and villages nearby is accelerated as commuters move outward, and access to the metropolitan market attracts new industry. The metropolis stimulates the region: the region in turn enlarges the market for the metropolis.

In Ontario the area around Toronto is growing at an incredible rate, linking the small manufacturing cities of the upper Grand Valley (Figure 3.5) to the metropolitan centres of Hamilton and Metro Toronto. New high-speed rail and highway links bring the fringes of the region closer to the core. Television, newspapers, cultural activities are available everywhere at the metropolitan level. Suddenly, once rurally-oriented towns like

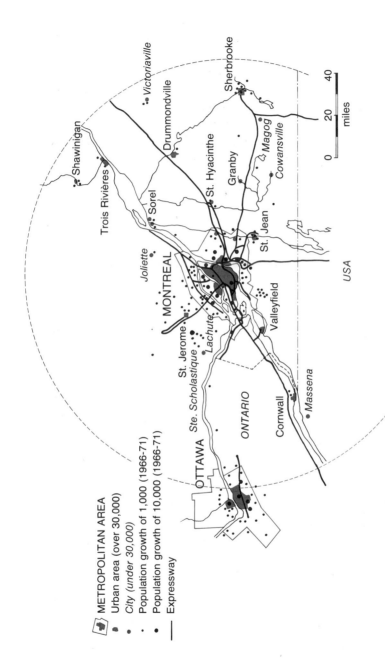

METROPOLITAN AREA

Urban area (over 30,000)

City (under 30,000)

• Population growth of 1,000 (1966–71)

● Population growth of 10,000 (1966–71)

—— Expressway

3.6　The Montreal Urban Field (100-mile radius)

Shawinigan

Trois Rivières

Sorel

Joliette

MONTREAL

St. Jerome

Ste. Scholastique

Lachute

Valleyfield

Massena

Cornwall

ONTARIO

OTTAWA

Victoriaville

Drummondville

St. Hyacinthe

Granby

Sherbrooke

Magog

Cowansville

St. Jean

USA

0   20   40

miles

Barrie, Bradford, Newcastle and Elora are full partners in urban Canada.

A kind of rejuvenation takes place in these towns. New young families, commuters, different kinds of businesses, stores, and factories, transform them within a few years. The city people can kid themselves for a while that these places combine access to the bright lights with rustic charm, until finally the roar of the expressways, the acres of stark new subdivisions, and the size of supermarket parking lots can no longer be ignored.

The role of such existing service centres in metropolitan growth is of considerable importance, for they help determine spatial patterns in the eventual metropolitan area. An existing town seems to be more attractive than either raw countryside or a totally new community. It provides a stable set of institutions for newcomers, and gives a sense of belonging. The scale, pace and layout of small towns are frequently attractive to city-dwellers. The problem is their transience. Given the recent urban growth rates, such places are gobbled up and transformed within a decade.

ARTHUR, Eric, *Toronto: No Mean City* (Toronto: University of Toronto Press, 1964). An architect's view of urban development.

CARELESS, J. M. S., "Frontierism, Metropolitanism, and Canadian History," *Canadian Historical Review* XXXV (March, 1954), pp. 1-21. A summary of the approaches to urbanism used by Canadian historians.

KERR, D. G. G. (ed.), *A Historical Atlas of Canada* (Toronto: Thomas Nelson & Sons (Canada) Ltd., 1960). Provides the context for understanding the development of the urban system.

PARKER, W. H., "The Towns of Lower Canada in the 1830s," in R. P. Beckinsale and J. M. Houston (eds.), *Urbanization and Its Problems* (Oxford: Basil Blackwell, 1968). Travellers' accounts of Quebec cities.

RADDALL, Thomas H., *Halifax, Warden of the North* (Toronto: McClelland and Stewart, 1971). One of the better histories of a particular city. However, virtually every town has at least one local history.

SPELT, Jacob, *The Urban Development of South-Central Ontario* (Assen, Netherlands: Van Gorcum, 1955, reprinted under the same title by McClelland and Stewart, 1972). Discusses the emergence of a system of small towns and cities between Toronto and Kingston.

WADE, Richard, *The Urban Frontier: The Rise of Western Cities, 1790-1830* (Cambridge: Harvard University Press, 1959). Argues for the important role of urban places in the settlement of the Midwest.

4 The Nation-City

Mainstreet, Downtown and Suburbia

The chapter title says it all. Canadians live in one big city, one of the largest in the world in total area, but closely integrated by a sophisticated and rapid communication network. Phones, planes, Telex, trucks, trains tie the various cities into a whole. Moreover, different parts of this nation-city perform specialized functions just as the different parts of real cities do; and the functions are analogous.

Urban Canada, for example, has one huge main drag, defined by the Trans-Canada Highway, the two major railway lines, the flight routes of the majority of the domestic carriers, and the United States border. Practically all of Canada's traffic takes at least a short trip on this main stem on its way to somewhere else.

Urban Canada also has a highly recognizable downtown which provides offices for the financial and business enterprises of the country; the rarer goods and services (T.V. programmes, entertainment, fashions, unusual machinery) unavailable at local shopping centres; and the heavy industry, diversified manufacturing, and major ports associated with large cities. This downtown is a composite, a twin-city called Montreal-Toronto; Montreal is analogous to the "real" downtown and Toronto to the fast developing, newer, uptown centre. The Maritimes might be seen as a somewhat decaying old city core —ports and warehouses and a transportation terminal, but overlooked now by developers seeking the active sites further uptown.

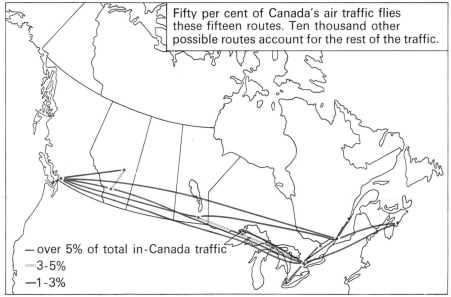

Fifty per cent of Canada's air traffic flies these fifteen routes. Ten thousand other possible routes account for the rest of the traffic.

— over 5% of total in-Canada traffic
····· 3-5%
—1-3%

Data obtained from Canadian Air Transport Board, *Origin and Destination Statistics, 1967* (Ottawa: 1968).

4.1   The "Main Drag": Most Travelled Air Routes

The West and North provide the nation's suburbs, newer and specialized in many different ways. Their agricultural, mining, and petroleum products flow into the central core of the country for processing. Their populations yield young men heading "downtown" to make their fortune. These people and products flow into Montreal-Toronto, to be put to work and then sent forth again, enriched and modified, to their suburban homes.

That is a little fanciful, but the absence of any significant downtown enterprises (special services, head offices, major industry) in these peripheral areas is a fact; and consequently the role the cities of these areas can play is very different from that of the downtown cities. And so Vancouver might be seen as the

67

last subway stop West, and Edmonton as the last one North; each with the cluster of activities that seems to make them almost independent centres but with their deepest reason for existence still the fact of their being at the end of the line—the line that leads downtown.

Like the communities and neighbourhoods in any city, Canadian cities perform two functions: a basic service function to the surrounding area (every region of Canada has its shopping centre); and a specialized function which provides a special reason for being (dormitory, warehouse, transportation terminal, industrial park, branch office, or institution).

The first of these roles—service—is highly competitive; the larger the area a city services, the bigger it becomes. So cities, like shopping centres, compete for the customer's trade. But the second role is complementary rather than competitive. A city, or a nation-city, needs administrative institutions—like Ottawa, or industrial complexes—like Sarnia; but it does not need more than one or two of these. Just as it would be uneconomical and redundant for a city to have two city halls or three zoos, so it is to have two Ottawas or two Sarnias, or too many Calgaries or Sudburies or Hamiltons.

It is the interlocking nature of these two kinds of networks —the action-reaction pattern of their associations—that ties Canada together into one nation, one nation-city.

Cities as Service Centres: The Competitive Network

The interrelationships of the nation-city make the economy of any one place highly dependent on its position vis-à-vis the rest. Earlier we pointed out regularities in the distribution of population size classes. The larger the city, the fewer places exist

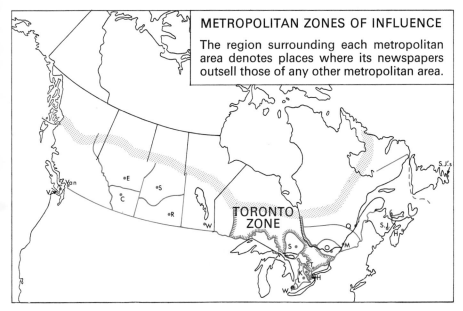

METROPOLITAN ZONES OF INFLUENCE

The region surrounding each metropolitan area denotes places where its newspapers outsell those of any other metropolitan area.

4.2 Trade Areas of Metropolitan Newspapers
Data obtained from the Audit Bureau of Circulation, 1968.

of similar size and the farther they are apart. This reflects the role of cities in serving the surrounding area. The larger the city, the larger the population of the trade area required to support it. Larger cities, however, serve in part the nearby smaller cities.

The services include the full range of consumer needs: stores for shopping, doctors and lawyers, and public services like schools and post offices. These activities are provided by a regular hierarchy of centres. The nearest small hamlet provides day-to-day needs for a farmer; the closest town is the source for weekly shopping; the city provides a wider choice for less frequently bought consumer items. The hierarchy may have several levels: the hamlet, village, town, city, metropolitan area. All centres of the same level offer the same kinds of services.

69

For example, George Thompson lives on a ranch in south-eastern Alberta. He frequents an unnamed crossroads along the Trans-Canada Highway for gas and cigarettes and takes his family into Brooks for groceries and haircuts. Periodically, he visits Medicine Hat to buy clothes and shoes for the kids, and each year tries to make a sortie to Calgary for Christmas shopping. Three or four times in his lifetime he has gone east to Toronto to bid on registered stock for his ranch.

The city-dweller comes into the chain at a higher level. He buys his cigarettes at the corner variety store, his groceries at the shopping plaza a mile or so away, and the kids' clothes downtown. This part of the hierarchy is contained within his own city. But occasionally he, too, likes to shop in a larger city where the variety is greater. People from Lindsay, Ontario, go frequently to Peterborough, 30 miles away, and occasionally to Toronto. Some Torontonians go now and again to New York or even to London, Paris, or Rome to buy those really distinctive labels.

The importance of the basic service function is shown by the uniformly high proportion of employment in these activities. Every metropolitan area employs about one-third of its male labour force in retailing and service activities which serve the townspeople and the surrounding countryside. This competitive trading role of cities divides up the whole of Canada's landscape into overlapping trade areas of different sizes. Each part of the country is served by a whole set of centres of different sizes. The Eastern Townships of Quebec, for instance, are served by Sherbrooke and by Montreal.

The trade areas in Figure 4.2 are defined for only one activity, the daily newspaper, and only for newspapers published within a Census Metropolitan Area. The pattern of trade areas will differ for each kind of product or service, although the patterns may be similar for many groups of activities. For example, buying groceries and going to the drug store are related activities (there is probably a drug store near your supermarket), but visiting a beer parlour may produce a quite different pattern, because it involves a different kind of customer who will undertake his trip at different times of the day.

Such generalizations are always being disturbed by the eccentricities of the consumer, who may purchase certain goods in unlikely places. A blouse bought in a fancy store in a larger centre may have much more appeal than a similar item found nearer home. Or, a city housewife may insist that eggs are "fresher" when bought from a certain roadside stand fifteen miles away, than the same product at Loblaw's.

Towns and cities which are particularly dependent on trade compete frantically with their neighbours to extend their trade areas. This competition, too, goes on at all levels of the hierarchy. Saskatchewan prairie towns compete for hospitals, police detachments, and licensed hotels. Ontario towns scramble for Brewers' Retail outlets and government liquor stores which attract new trade from smaller places.

Some notable larger and continuing competitions are those between the ports of the eastern seaboard. Halifax and Saint John strive against each other and together fight the main threat: Montreal. They resisted the St. Lawrence Seaway for years and now they annually fight any move to keep Montreal free of winter ice. The traffic at such ports brings with it shipping, wholesaling and processing firms, and helps generate a large retail and service trade.

In Central Canada, Toronto and Montreal are the heavyweight contenders for the right to dominate the national financial and corporate headquarters market. Neither has won and the battle continues, extending into other areas as well. The Toronto papers are filled with self-congratulation when downtown Toronto gets a new building, but despondent at the success of the Métro and big-league baseball in Montreal.

The rivalry between Edmonton and Calgary is famous. These two cities compete for everything: trade, industry, government investment, winning football teams, local politicians, population, and the image of sophistication. Edmonton is larger, but Calgary has the Stampede. If Edmonton is the gateway to the north, then Calgary is the gateway to the Rockies. And so it goes. It seems childish, but fortunes and political power come with urban growth. Once dominant in a region, a city is virtually never overtaken, but a series of defeats in these kinds of endeavour may destroy a city's reputation for growth, or as a town where things keep happening.

Cities Serving the Nation: The Complementary Network

The non-service activities—mining, industry, transportation, government, or education—are the specialties which characterize and individualize the particular economy of a city. In the hierarchical system of service activities, towns interact only with larger or smaller places which have different levels of service, but these specialized activities, different for each town, lead to relationships between all urban centres in the network. The goods produced in each place complement each other. Belleville and Kingston, for instance, provide basically the same retail outlets and services for their trade areas; they compete for business at the margins of the trade areas, but they have different and complementary roles in the national economy. Belleville has a series of small manufacturing plants, whose products are shipped throughout the country. An important function for Kingston is the support of a number of government institutions. The federal government maintains a penitentiary which requires 500 workers, and also supports the Royal Military College. The province underwrites a major university with 2,000 workers and 6,500 inmates.

4.3

Economic Roles of Canadian Cities

A city's location on this chart indicates the extent and direction of its economic specialization. Note that most cities are clustered together; there are few extremes. There is little variation among cities in the proportion of workers in tertiary activities; the proportion of industrial and other activities, however, varies more widely from city to city. Note that the largest centres are nearest the median.

100%

TRADE,
SERVICES,
FINANCE

★ Metropolitan Areas

• Other cities > 30,000

OTHER SPECIAL
ACTIVITIES
(Transport, Public
Service, Defence)

100%

WESTERN
SERVICE
CENTRES

THE CONNECTING LINKS

★ Saskatoon
★ St. John's
Regina ★   ★ Edmonton
Winnipeg ★ Calgary ★ Moncton
Vancouver ★ ★ Saint John ★ Victoria   ★ Halifax
London ★   • Kingston   ★ Ottawa
Sherbrooke ★ ★ Trois Rivières   ★ Quebec
Toronto ★ ★ Montreal St. Jerome   • Lakehead
Chicoutimi-Jonquière • ★ Kitchener • Niagara Falls
Windsor • ★ Brampton   • Valleyfield
Peterborough • • Hamilton • Sydney
Brantford • ★ Guelph • St. Jeans • Sault Ste. Marie
Drummondville • • Shawinigan
St. Catharines • Sudbury
• Timmins   • Welland
• Oshawa

EASTERN INDUSTRIAL TOWNS

RESOURCE
EXPLOITATION
AND INDUSTRY

100%

Data obtained from Statistics Canada, *Census of Canada, 1961.*

The role of service centre tends to generate a uniform network of cities spread more or less evenly across the nation, like the regular dot pattern of Saskatchewan towns. The specialized economic activities, however, generate a variety of distributions. Transportation systems—waterways, railroads, highways —lead to a succession of towns strung out along the route. Resource exploitation activities—lumbering, mining, fishing, hydro-electric developments—generate clusters of towns spread out along the fringe of settlement.

Figure 4.3 describes the employment patterns of the larger Canadian cities. The service activities—trade, construction, transportation and public service—are fairly stable, with each city having roughly the same proportion of each. The areas of specialization, resource industries and manufacturing, show much greater variation. Except for the mining-based cities of Sudbury and Timmins, no other place has more than 10 per cent of its work force employed in these activities. The percentage of the work force in manufacturing varies from 5.8 per cent (Timmins) to 60.7 per cent (Oshawa).

Transportation and government activities usually are just part of a city's services but occasionally they play a very important role. Ottawa, of course, has a large government work force, but so too have the combined military bases and provincial capitals, Halifax and Victoria. Transportation activities support the ports of St. John's, Saint John and Moncton; the railroad junctions of Winnipeg and the West; and the major transfer point of the lakehead.

Be it railroad centre, mill town, provincial capital or mining town, the specialized economic base is an important aspect of the city's individuality. Compare the steelworkers of Hamilton, the merchants of Lethbridge or Saskatoon, and the executives of Toronto; different incomes, ethnic groups and values, patterns of growth, are the products of this diversity.

Many of our city images spring from these different economic roles. We think of Peterborough and Quaker Oats,

Kingston and the penitentiary, Saint John and K. C. Irving, Thunder Bay and the grain elevator.

Flows Linking Cities

The competition and complementarity of the cities' economies depend on close communication. Goods, money, information, people, must flow readily among places. Decisions from Ottawa, capital from Toronto, automobiles from Oshawa and Windsor flow throughout the country.

The amount of inter-urban traffic is reflected in the transportation and communication networks of Canada. Most of the traffic and all of the main routes link major urban places. Business executives maintain close contact with their colleagues in other cities, and white-collar workers migrate from city to city at the whim of their employers. Manufacturing products are conceived here, assembled there, and consumed somewhere else in the network.

In terms of time or cost, the metropolitan nodes are more accessible to each other than to parts of their own service areas. Certainly many kinds of movements and relationships are more likely to take place among the cities than between a city and its rural hinterland. Toronto and Montreal are an hour apart by air (airport to airport), less than 4 hours by the Turbo train. Many businessmen go down for the day. Telex, trunk telephone links, air and rail service, and trucking services attract shipments of goods or information from the city's service area, channel them between two cities and then deliver them out from the destination. Urban places are in continuous, immediate contact. Rural areas are compelled to use the urban network in order to link rural Alberta to rural New Brunswick. The movement is from country to city to city to country.

4.4 Accessibility of Canadian Metropolitan Areas
(Hours apart by fastest means of public transport, city centre to city centre.)

	Calgary	Edmonton	Halifax	Hamilton	Kitchener	London	Montreal	Ottawa	Quebec	Regina	St. John's	Saint John	Saskatoon	Sudbury	Toronto	Vancouver	Victoria	Windsor	Winnipeg	RANKED ACCESSIBILITY
Calgary	—	3	9	6	6	8	7	7	9	4	13	10	4	8	6	4	5	7	4	8
Edmonton	3	—	9	6	6	7	7	8	8	4	14	11	4	9	6	6	4	5	6	9
Halifax	9	9	—	5	5	7	3	3	5	11	3	3	11	8	5	11	13	8	8	15
Hamilton	6	6	5	—	2	4	3	3	5	6	7	6	6	4	1	7	8	4	5	1
Kitchener	6	6	5	2	—	3	5	6	7	8	7	6	4	2	2	8	8	4	5	3
London	8	7	7	4	3	—	4	5	6	9	8	6	9	5	3	10	10	3	6	7
Montreal	7	7	3	3	5	4	—	3	3	8	4	5	8	5	3	8	9	5	5	4
Ottawa	7	8	3	3	6	5	3	—	4	8	6	6	9	5	3	9	9	5	5	5
Quebec	9	8	5	5	7	6	3	4	—	9	6	5	12	6	5	12	14	7	8	12
Regina	4	4	11	6	8	9	8	8	9	—	13	12	3	9	6	6	6	9	3	16
St. John's	13	14	3	7	7	8	4	6	6	13	—	7	13	10	7	9	16	10	11	19
Saint John	10	11	3	6	6	6	5	6	5	12	7	—	10	9	6	12	13	9	8	17
Saskatoon	4	4	11	6	4	9	8	9	12	3	13	10	—	8	6	5	7	8	4	13
Sudbury	8	9	8	4	2	5	5	5	6	9	10	9	8	—	3	9	9	5	5	11
Toronto	6	6	5	1	2	3	3	3	5	6	7	6	6	3	—	7	8	3	5	1
Vancouver	4	6	11	7	8	10	8	9	12	6	9	12	5	9	7	—	3	9	5	14
Victoria	5	4	13	8	8	10	9	9	14	6	16	13	7	9	8	3	—	14	6	18
Windsor	7	5	8	4	4	3	5	5	7	9	10	9	8	5	3	9	14	—	6	10
Winnipeg	4	6	8	5	5	6	5	5	8	3	11	8	4	5	5	5	6	6	—	6
TOTAL	120	123	139	86	87	111	95	102	130	140	166	142	133	127	86	137	165	125	105	
RANK ORDER	8	9	15	1	3	7	4	5	12	16	19	17	13	11	1	14	18	10	6	

Data obtained from Air Canada timetable on North American services, March 21 - April 29, 1969.

Figure 4.4 illustrates many of these points. First, note how close all the metropolitan areas are to one another. The greatest travel time, between Victoria and St. John's, Newfoundland, is sixteen hours. Toronto and Montreal are within nine hours of any metropolitan area in the country. Secondly, note how the "main drag" effect channels traffic through the very largest centres. If the total accessibility is considered, larger peripheral places like Winnipeg are easier to reach than smaller, more central places like London or Sudbury. Both distance and size of place (which correlates with frequency of flights) are important.

The "main drag" in practice is evident in figure 4.1, which shows the concentration of actual movement in the narrow East-West band of metropolitan areas. Within the urban band a series of physical, political and cultural barriers concentrates movement within regions and lessens the nation-wide links. The long expanse of the Canadian Shield separating Winnipeg and Toronto reduces links between Central Canada and the West. To a lesser extent, the Rockies separate Vancouver from the prairie cities.

In the East, the long northern thumb of Maine separates the Maritimes cities from any intensive contact with Ontario and Quebec. There is also a cultural barrier. For certain kinds of contact, French-speaking cities act as quite different entities. The flow of messages and migrants between English and French city centres is markedly lower than would normally be expected. French-Canadian cities are largely restricted in their contacts to other French-Canadian centrès in Quebec and the neighbouring provinces of Ontario and New Brunswick. Hence the relatively inaccessible nature of Quebec City, which ranks in Figure 4.4 between Sudbury and Saskatoon.

The location of the two dominant urban areas, Toronto and Montreal, is the biggest factor in determining flows within Canada. They concentrate interaction within a small part of the country. Movement takes place between the West and

Central Canada, and the Maritimes and Central Canada, but not across the nation. Toronto is Mecca for Newfies and Bluenoses; Calgary, Edmonton and Vancouver are filled with expatriates from Ottawa, Toronto and Hamilton; but the longer jump from Cape Breton to Vancouver is seldom made.

If this pattern seems like a natural state of affairs, compare it with the pattern of the United States, where New York and Los Angeles, the two leading metropolitan areas, are located at the opposite ends of the continent. Continuous movement takes place between the two. East coast and West coast styles and attitudes dominate the central area of the country.

These patterns of interaction, as well as other kinds of movement—the flow of goods or migrants, for instance—taking place among cities, have considerable political implications. The degree to which all Canadian metropolitan areas are linked together in commerce and social interaction determines the degree to which the major regions of the country are tied together functionally. All this provides the rationale for continued nationhood. If we find that the cities of British Columbia are becoming less closely tied to Toronto and Montreal, are building stronger contacts with Seattle or Portland, then political allegiance may ultimately be expected to shift. Similarly, the more integrated the economic functions of Ontario and Quebec, the greater the political stress they can overcome.

We can only conjecture, though, what the role of Canadian cities is within the larger North American city system. It can be argued that Montreal and Toronto are subject to New York in the larger hierarchy and that their relative success is due to access to the American network and market rather than to a response to the Canadian environment. In this sense urban Canada is a peripheral part of a large North American urban network.

The Growth of Cities Within the Network

The growth of each city depends on the combination of activities it undertakes for the national economy. World markets affect the resource towns like Timmins or Elliot Lake; the agricultural prosperity of the surrounding region controls the fate of prairie market towns like Moose Jaw and Brandon. The centres for political administration—Ottawa, Victoria, Fredericton—grow inexorably, in good times and in bad.

Close ties among cities also make each of them highly dependent on the others; more dependent, in many ways, than on the activities within their own regions. The cities form a tightly interlocking system. If Calgary attracts new industries at an unusual rate, those firms may have been diverted from Edmonton or Regina and those cities will grow less rapidly. At any rate, people in Drumheller or Swift Current who once found the other cities to be attractive places to shop may switch to a larger, more exciting Calgary. And as Calgary grows its linkages with other cities increase. More people fly between Calgary and Lethbridge, Calgary and Vancouver. The size of the Calgary market increases so that more goods are shipped in from Winnipeg, Toronto and Montreal.

Each economic change, be it national growth, provincial policy, or expansion of the world wheat market, has direct impact on some part of the urban network. As Canada grows the federal government builds a new post office in St. John's and IBM decides to set up new regional offices in Sudbury and Sherbrooke. The growth of the provincial economy forces Saskatchewan to build a new university in Regina. Grain sales mean more grain-handlers at the lakehead, more stockbrokers in Winnipeg.

But if the trade area of Owen Sound does not grow and generate new stores, if the national and provincial growth is centred in some other area of the province, if no new factories come in, and the government builds no hospitals or schools, the city remains as it always has; the streets and utilities, the housing and stores, grow older. There is no incentive to build new institutions, create new organizations. The more ambitious young people drift off to the opportunities created by growth elsewhere.

Many Canadian cities are completely dependent on the world commodity markets—for newsprint, or rapeseed, or codfish—and on the pattern of linkages they have with surrounding places. A major wheat sale or a new expressway can spell prosperity or disaster for a city. Both are far beyond its control.

The best policy for survival has always been diversification. The greater variety of activities a city has, the less dependent it is on any one of them, and the less vulnerable it is to a single trend or decision made several thousand miles away. Oromocto depends on defense department decisions. St. Thomas, on the other hand, grew out of railroad refueling and crew resting procedures, but has since diversified its economic base.

Alternatively, another strategy is to grow. Larger cities are more diverse economically, and they also serve a larger region. If the local mine runs out of ore, one nearby or a new pulp mill may take up the slack.

Very few cities have continued to grow while based on the same function. Calgary, originally a police and administrative centre, became the service centre and shipping point for the cattle country—and then, suddenly, the headquarters for the Canadian petroleum industry. Peterborough, a rural service centre, slowly built up its industrial base and now with its university is becoming a regional centre for government and tourist activities.

80

Traditionally, industry was the best way for specialized cities to diversify and expand. Service centres tried to attract market-oriented factories, and resource-based towns pleaded for more on-site processing. Recently, a variety of government activities has proven equally valuable. If your MP can convince Ottawa of the need for an air force base, or a veteran's hospital, or research facilities, several hundred jobs in the civil service will be provided, which will be well-nigh permanent. Similarly the province might be coerced into building a mental hospital or university.

The immediate objective for most small cities is more jobs of any kind, jobs to reduce local unemployment and keep the young people from leaving. The industrial commissioners and town councils of rapidly growing cities are more particular; they know that most new employees will be newcomers to the city, and they seek out firms employing high-income professional people, in industries which will continue to grow and innovate. Slow-growth cities will take anything—run-down textile firms or plastic assembling plants employing unskilled persons at the minimum legal wage.

As cities grow larger the service role and the specializations become more and more intertwined. Toronto and Montreal provide financial, administrative, and cultural services for the whole country, and produce manufactured goods as well. Vancouver, Winnipeg and Halifax perform the same tasks for their regions while also serving national functions.

BOURNE, L. S. and MacKINNON, R. D. (eds.), *Urban Systems Development in Central Canada,* University of Toronto, Department of Geography Research Publication No. 9 (Toronto: 1972). A series of essays describing the patterns and processes operating among the cities of Ontario and Quebec.

KERR, Donald, "Metropolitan Dominance in Canada," in John Warkentin (ed.), *Canada: A Geographical Interpretation* (Toronto: Methuen, 1968). A look at the Canadian metropolitan areas and their linkages.

MASTERS, Donald C., "Toronto Versus Montreal: The Struggle for Financial Hegemony, 1680-1875," *Canadian Historical Review,* XXII (1941) pp. 133-146. This study is updated by Donald Kerr, "Some Aspects of the Geography of Finance in Canada," *Canadian Geographer* IV, 4 (1965), pp. 175-192.

MATHESON, Marion H., "The Hinterlands of Saint John," *Geographical Bulletin,* VII (1955), pp. 65-102. A comprehensive study of the areas served for different goods.

MAXWELL, J. W., GREIG, J. A. and MEYER, H. G., "The Functional Structure of Canadian Cities." In *Readings in Canadian Geography,* edited by R. M. Irving, 2nd ed. (Toronto: Holt, Rinehart and Winston, 1972), pp. 150-167. Using measures of the employment structure, cities are grouped into functional types.

MURDIE, Robert A., "Cultural Differences in Consumer Travel," *Economic Geography,* XLI (July, 1965), pp. 211-233. Which farmer goes to which town? Murdie shows differences between Mennonites and non-Mennonites in the Kitchener area.

PERRY, Robert L., *Galt U.S.A.* (Toronto: The Financial Post, 1972). A look at a small manufacturing city—and who runs it.

PROVINCE OF SASKATCHEWAN, Royal Commission on Agriculture and Rural Life, *Service Centres,* Report No. 12 (Queen's Printer: Regina, 1957). The trading areas for southwestern Saskatchewan towns are described and analyzed in detail.

ROBINSON, Ira M., *New Industrial Towns on Canada's Resource Frontier* (Chicago: University of Chicago, Department of Geography, Research Series No. 73, 1962). A study of the planned community in the North.

5 Shaping the Form of a City

The City Nation

Each city in Urban Canada is Canada in miniature. Most of the significant processes of social change, the national problems, are manifest in Moncton or Brandon or Lethbridge. Examining these problems on a city scale makes them visible and identifiable.

As you watch the high-rises climb in the blocks around you, or see the kids playing in the condemned buildings of the urban renewal area, or observe the clash of cultures in the supermarket, the abstract issues of Parliament and the press become real. Each commonplace political decision about throughways or subways or water pipelines, or the nature of a metropolitan government, recreates on a smaller scale the debates of the Fathers of Confederation.

Growth is a national phenomenon, but it's happening in the cities. Virtually every city recognizes the implications of rapid growth: more jobs, but higher taxes for new public services; investments predicated on the promise of continual expansion; blight or obsolescence as old facilities become inadequate; new jobs and promotions, but a chance of being uprooted from your neighbourhood.

Regional disparity is an urban problem also. By and large, the provinces with booming cities are rich, the provinces with an agricultural or fishing base are lagging. And the city's own attempts to deal with the gap between slum area and rich district repeat exactly the efforts of federal cabinet ministers to redistribute wealth. To understand the problems of the poorer regions a city-dweller has only to stroll through the poor parts of his own city. The differences between rich and poor, young and old, liberals and conservatives, French and English speaking inhabitants, the old WASPs and the new immigrants: all are sharply focussed within individual Candian cities.

In this sense all Canadian cities are similar; all reflect a common culture and its problems. And the common culture produces a common form. All Canadian cities have stores, parks and houses; and all have some kind of economic base: port, factory, smelter or government buildings. As they grow, cities produce new activities and new buildings for the activities, but again the activities and structures are similar from city to city: expressways and airports; specialized income and ethnic communities; suburbs where families of similar age cluster together; a used car golden mile and a pawnbrokers' row.

Developers, consumers, entrepreneurs, politicians: all combine to create a city. Why do regular patterns emerge? Because the possible choices of each individual in the pattern-making process are severely limited by both his own culture and the cultural context of his decision. How many choices does a 35-year-old Canadian housebuyer with three children and an income of $15,000 have? His choices are even more limited if, say, his wife insists on a particular school.

As a result, Victoria and Kitchener, for example, despite the peculiarities of their settings and economic roles, have very much in common. Both have grown within a market economy, with a typical Canadian municipal government. Any of us could locate a shoe store or city hall in either of them.

The same kinds of forces that we have already seen shaping constraints on the development of the nation are those that affect the forms of Canadian cities: the sequence of growth, the physical environment, and the economic, political, and cultural forces which all Canadian cities share.

84

The Development Process

At each stage in a city's growth, decisions are made within the physical and cultural environment of that point in time, while previous developments within the city adjust to a larger population, or income increases, or the spread of automobiles.

The earliest settlers located the initial core of the city and no matter what the original *raison d'être*—fort, trading post, river crossing, sawmill—all future growth takes place outward from this point. The city centre may shift inland with time as it has in Toronto or Montreal, but not very far—a few hundred yards, perhaps a mile. The imprint of the first activity remains on the city structure.

And so does the pattern of the first roads: the settlement roads such as Yonge Street, and the early trails, originally designed to link small villages but now providing arterial roads for large cities—the MacLeod Trail in Calgary, Kingston Road in Toronto, Hamilton Road in London.

The original pattern of settlement as determined by the lot size and the survey procedures used to locate the concession roads, eventually evolves into the city's street system. In parts of Quebec the long strips of farms touching the rivers have led to rows of secondary roads each paralleling the waterway. This causes complicated traffic problems where rivers meet.

The early trails extended settlement out in long arms toward nearby towns. Gridded road patterns were used to fill in between the extensions at later stages in city growth. Finally the expressways cutting across the older patterns have produced new nodal developments: activities which cluster around expressway interchanges, such as shopping centres, trucking firms, and light industrial plants.

All future decisions about the city's form are made in the context of this initial shape determined in the first period of

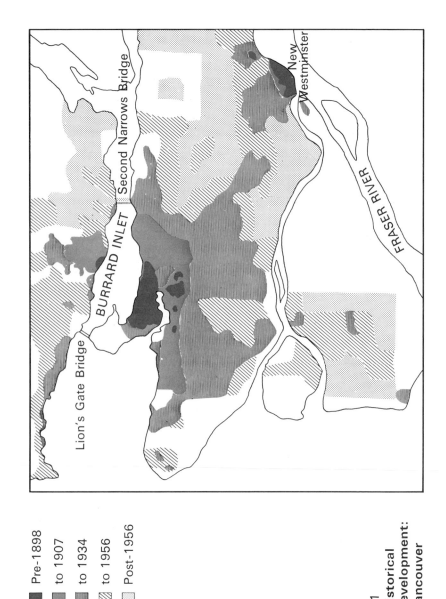

Pre-1898
to 1907
to 1934
to 1956
Post-1956

Lion's Gate Bridge

BURRARD INLET

Second Narrows Bridge

New Westminster

FRASER RIVER

5.1
Historical
Development:
Vancouver

settlement. Today's developer lays out street plans on a lot surveyed a hundred years ago, with the size of pre-urban farms defining the block patterns. Every Canadian city contains adjacent subdivisions which are barely in contact with one another because they were built on two different farms and developed independently a year or so apart.

The developer himself identifies the appropriate set of land uses for his property, making his decisions from his knowledge of his own environment. How much capital can he raise? What is the market for industrial or commercial land? How many people will live in the city in twenty years? What public services are available now and in the immediate future? What kind of zoning control exists over the property?

The developer may be wrong, misled by the optimism of civic leaders or unaware of other developments presently underway. Pressed for time or funds, he may choose the simplest or easiest alternative, the one with the quickest return rather than the greatest long-run profit, but his decision—to build a gas station or high-rise apartment, to lay out lots for $15,000 or $50,000 houses—will mark the city for the next fifty years.

Within the developer's plan entrepreneurs take over the site and construct the buildings. Again, future needs of the city are interpreted by individuals who desire, first of all, to make a profit. Construction decisions are determined by the specific requirements of the activities of the initial occupants: the X-Y shirt factory, a hardware store, or the Smith family which has six girls, two boys and a dog; and also by the current building code, capital market, technology, and pattern of consumer preferences. Soundproofing and open plans are important in the seventies, but ninety years ago it was high ceilings and stained-glass windows that caught the buyers.

This initial basic structure, the physical layout of the site and buildings, is continuously modified by the establishments which use it thereafter. A cigar store replaces the hardware

SETTING

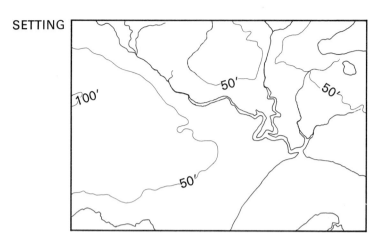

TRANSPORTATION
ROUTES

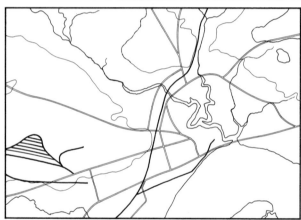

INSTITUTIONAL
AND MAJOR
LAND USE
ELEMENTS

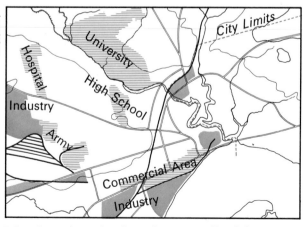

5.2   **Context of a Development Decision**

store; the X-Y company turns to plastic mouldings instead of shirts; and the Smith family grows up, moves out, and is replaced by a little old lady with seven boarders. If the city continues to grow, more severe forms of redevelopment take place. Houses are converted to offices and stores, and ultimately torn down for high-rise, office-commercial developments. Other houses are subdivided into flats or rooming houses, and small apartment buildings emerge in vacant lots.

In the older part of the city, the separate ownership of lot-size parcels of land is one of the greatest barriers to private and public redevelopment. To build a new apartment or plan a group of stores in order to take advantage of scale economies and technological change, requires years of painstaking land assembly involving dozens of individual owners.

At the outskirts of the city, however, the scale of development has increased over time. Sites of a square mile or more are built up at one time. Whole neighbourhoods and whole shopping centres are laid out as parts of a single project. The curved streets are planned, the utilities are installed, the traffic patterns are anticipated as integral parts of the development process.

Physical Constraints

Most major Canadian cities occupy distinctive settings which are responsible, at least in part, for the unique characteristics of these places. It is not just the physical presence of the ocean or cliff or river valley which distinguishes them, but the impact of these physical phenomena on the sequence of development and the location of various economic activities. Toronto, for instance, ignores the lake and is rapidly filling its ravines with asphalt, but the hidden waterfront and the covered-over river valleys have already left their imprints on the pattern of districts, streets, and buildings.

Most notable is the role of physical features as barriers to development, segregating land uses and social groups, preventing interaction between spatially adjacent areas, and holding back growth for decades until a bridge or tunnel suddenly transforms the access pattern of the whole area. Vancouver, trapped between the ocean inlets and the mountains, provides a good example. Growth began at three separate sites: New Westminster on the Fraser River, Gastown just east of the current downtown on Burrard Inlet, and across the inlet around a sawmill complex in what is now North Vancouver. Transportation linked them together: a ferry across Burrard Inlet, and a highway from Vancouver to New Westminster. The construction of Lion's Gate Bridge in 1938 encouraged the rapid growth of West Vancouver, and the recent completion of the new bridge across the second narrows permits the rapid expansion of the northeast shore.

In the same way one could look at the relationships between growth and form in connection with Quebec and the St. Lawrence, Edmonton and the Saskatchewan River. Of all the metropolitan areas, only Regina, on its plain with no major water features, is in complete control of terrain. Wascana Creek could have been readily converted to a sewer. Instead it was turned into a lake and made a focal point of the landscape.

The effect of terrain in separating areas early in the settlement stage may lead to several commercial cores in the structure of the present metropolitan area. Two places on either side of an inlet each act as centres for the surrounding area since they are perhaps an hour's travel apart. Suddenly a bridge or tunnel puts them two minutes apart or metropolitan growth surrounds both of them with miles of suburbs, and you have a single city with two nuclei: Halifax-Dartmouth.

No single land use is characteristic of a certain kind of site, although certain regularities do exist. Residential and recreational activities are the most likely to locate on extremely rugged terrain. Retail and industrial enterprises seek flat, open land.

Some of the most attractive urban sites are occupied by the bread-and-butter activities, the railroads or the mills, a phenomenon stemming from earlier periods of development. The mills were the first of the industrial developments and required water access. The first railroads, out of their economic dominance, could run tracks through the choicest parts of the cityscape, along the shorelines in many cities such as Sarnia, Windsor and Toronto, or cutting through the centre of the city as in London or Calgary. The same forces of economic necessity have decorated Hamilton Bay with the steel mill, and for years lighted the night view from Parliament Hill in Ottawa with the Swan Toilet Tissue sign on the pulp mill across the river.

Only in the last few years have the residents of the city been able to compete for the amenities of these choice sites. Residential subdivisions and high-rise apartments are seeking out water-edge or ravine-side locations. Cities are slowly, very slowly, recognizing the importance of such areas for recreation and open space.

But for many of these once attractive areas the awareness comes too late. The shorelines have been filled in and lined with docks and warehouses, now decaying, or with weed-strewn freight yards. And the ravines have received the garbage of generations of citizens.

Marketplace Constraints

The process of development is shaped by three sets of institutions: the marketplace, the government, and the household. The wants, the values, the patterns of behaviour of individuals and families are satisfied or manipulated by a wide

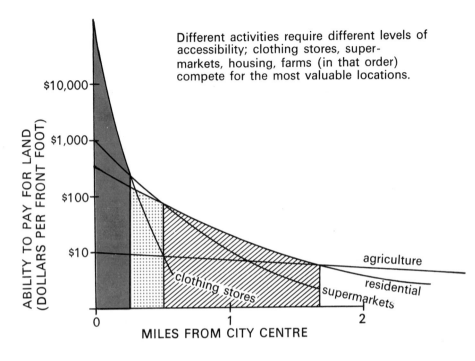

Different activities require different levels of accessibility; clothing stores, supermarkets, housing, farms (in that order) compete for the most valuable locations.

5.3 Land Values and Land Use

range of commercial activities and institutions operating for profit, and by numerous non-profit governmental institutions designed to satisfy specific kinds of group demands. If we think of the city as an artifact, an artificial creation of man, then we realize that we get what we want—after our wants are filtered by institutional processes.

A private enterprise or market economy has a great many implications for urban form, some good, some bad, depending on the point of view. Certainly it leads to diversity, a tremendous variety of activities and life styles: the crazy-quilt architecture along a city street, the fantastic array of stores, each selling a different kind of goods, and all the different kinds of jobs available. On the other hand, many of these possible activities, such as prostitution, or sidewalk cafés, or junkyards in residential areas, are frowned upon by certain areas of society, and the public sector takes steps to deter them.

The marketplace exerts several constraints as well. You can't abandon downtown; too many merchants have investments there. You can't build a park in this area; the land is too valuable. You can't put public housing in our neighbourhood; it will lower the value of our property. The resultant continuous friction between elements of the market economy and various public institutions is one of the fascinating aspects of urban life.

Ideally the market acts to sort things out, to transmit to developers and entrepreneurs the needs of the populace. A developer's experience in building and selling homes, for instance, gives him a great deal of insight into what the public is prepared to pay for. For a fixed price increase should he improve the landscaping, or build in a garbage disposal unit?

The same kind of costing process allocates activities over space. Property values vary widely throughout the city. In the best downtown location in Montreal or Toronto land is worth up to $10,000 per front foot, while in the furthest, undeveloped, unserviced part of the urban fringe it may be as low as $10. Within this spectrum each activity chooses a location according to its requirements.

The predominant source of land value variation is access. Stores dependent on passersby for customers are willing to pay the greatest amount for a site, and garbage dumps or junkyards pay the least. The result is a regular grouping of activities in space. Activities needing contact with other activities are found close together near the city centre. Others go to the periphery where land is cheaper.

Land costs within the city centre correspond to movement at the pedestrian scale. They may fluctuate widely within a

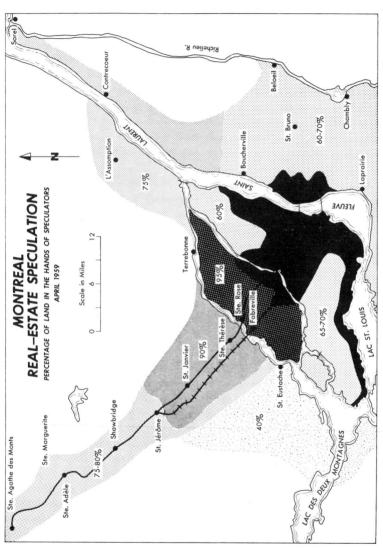

5.4 Speculation in Land: Montreal

Claude Langlois, "Problems of Urban Growth in Greater Montreal," *The Canadian Geographer*, V. 3 (Autumn, 1961), pp. 1–11. Reproduced by permission of the author.

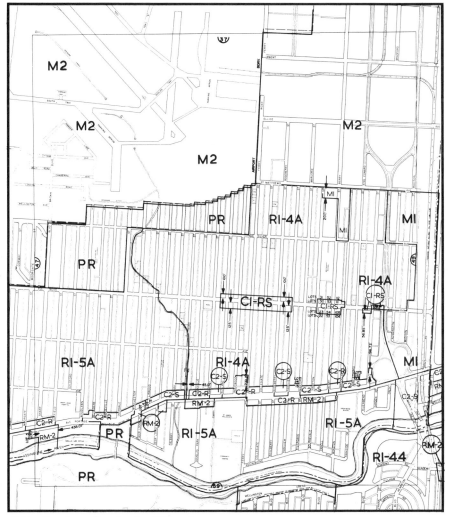

5.5 Zoning Controls: Winnipeg

A municipal by-law defines permitted land uses in each part of the city.

REGULAR DISTRICTS

PR	PARK—RECREATIONAL
R1-5A	ONE FAMILY RESIDENTIAL
R1-44	" " "
R1-4A	" " "
RM-2	MULTIPLE FAMILY RESIDENTIAL

C1-RS	NEIGHBORHOOD RETAIL SERVICE
C2-R	COMMUNITY RETAIL
C2-S	COMMUNITY SERVICE
M1	LIMITED INDUSTRIAL
M2	" "

METROPOLITAN CORPORATION OF GREATER WINNIPEG
PLANNING DIVISION

short distance. In Winnipeg, for instance, two main department stores—Eaton's and the Hudson's Bay—are located on the south side of Portage Avenue. The frontage between them is the best retail location in the city, but on the north side of this extremely wide street pedestrian traffic and land values are much lower and quite different kinds of stores are found.

The market also controls the pressures for development and redevelopment. Speculators, anticipating city growth and a continued rise in land values, buy farmland at the edge of the city and sell it to developers as needed. Within the city, once all the vacant land is used, the land supporting the activity which can least afford to pay high rents is redeveloped. Apartment-house developers buy up and demolish single-family buildings. Office buildings gobble up old stores. Low-density activities which cannot pay for high accessibility are continuously pushed outward as the city grows.

Public Sector Constraints

In order to complement and modify the activities of the marketplace the citizens as a whole take action through a great variety of public institutions. The different levels of government have each traditionally specialized in certain services which can be more economically or equitably provided by a single institution. The effects of these service activities provide another set of constraints on city form.

The city itself, for instance, can impose public policy on its development pattern by encouraging or directing growth through the provision of services such as transportation or water or sewers. The power of withholding these activities may even be used to enforce zoning and other planning controls which seek to restrict certain kinds of activities.

Potentially the investment decision about public services is the most powerful form of public control, but the implications for growth of such decisions are not always visible, and even less often considered. Frequently such decisions simply reflect administrative or engineering problems within a single department: the last-minute whittling back of a departmental budget, or the dimensions of a water main built in 1911.

Development of a given site for a given activity depends on access—a function of the transportation network—and public services: schools, water, sewage. When a new expressway or subway or bridge or tunnel is constructed, patterns of access throughout the city change radically. Land values are forced to adjust, and soon activities move and modify the landscape. New industry springs up along the urban bypass. New apartments rise along the subway. New residential subdivisions wait on the extension of the sewage network, or the construction of a new school.

And yet, by and large, it is not these powerful public service bodies that are most directly and visibly concerned with the sequence and arrangement of development, but the official city planning agency. Zoning, subdivision control, urban renewal and assorted other activities are directed at the improvement of the urban landscape, primarily by controlling activities of the market. A typical zoning by-law restricts the kinds of activities which can locate in each area of the city, attempting to reduce the costs to some parts of the community (nearby homeowners) resulting from the profits of other members (gas station owners).

Unfortunately, the planning process, lacking any kind of economic lever, is not very effective when it comes into conflict with the powerful forces of the market. The desires for money gain and the fears of money loss soon coalesce into powerful political pressure.

In Canada, a country of very rapid urban growth and change, there is a tolerance for almost any aesthetic nightmare, a feeling that "it's only temporary" or "it could be worse." Only a virtually unanimous set of values held by the citizens, accompanied by a powerful sense of outrage, can modify the private landscape. Urban Canada, at the moment, has neither.

Patterns of Behaviour

With all their imperfections, the marketplace and the government operate for the needs of the population. The urban landscape reflects the physical, social, and cultural requirements of the citizens themselves. The single-family box is not thrust upon us by some dictatorial force; it is lovingly sought after by a large body of the population who seek from it economic security, privacy, and independence.

The form of the city is the product of an integrated and complex culture. Ponder the implications for city form of such things as the tradition of the family, the separation of home and work, and the willingness to commute. The Canadian allocations of time to different activities—to shopping, to recreation inside and outside the home—affect the quantity, type and spacing of stores and parks, the design of houses and subdivisions, the size and location of parking lots, movie theatres, and gas stations.

It is impossible, of course, to survey here all the possible patterns of behaviour that affect the form of our cities. Even a look at Canadian sexual habits has its relevance for street design (remember those cruising car pickups?). One method of exploring the sociological causes of city form is an examination of daily patterns of movement.

Gradually we are gaining more information about movement patterns, their distance, direction, mode of travel and time of day. Although the total number of trips made tends to decline regularly with distance, the direction of the trips is

- 1-3
△ 4-10
□ 11-25
◄ 26-50
● 51-100
■ 101-200
☆ 201-400
★ 401-800
✪ 800+

5.6 **Daily Movement Patterns: London** *(Patterns of travel by one household in London, Ontario: number of times a given point is traversed in fourteen weeks)*

James W. Simmons, "An Urban Information Field," *Ontario Geography*, No. 2 (1968). (London, Ontario: University of Western Ontario, Department of Geography.) Reproduced by courtesy of the author and *Ontario Geography*.

often biased strongly towards one or two sectors, the city centre or the place of work. Before there was much information it was assumed that the trip patterns were quite simple; people went to the nearest store, bought houses near their jobs, and so on. Recent studies indicate that patterns are extremely complex. Housewives visit two or three widely separated shopping plazas within a week.

People are increasingly mobile within urban areas, ranging far afield to work or shop or visit. It is no longer possible to equate nearness with actual contact. High-rise apartment dwellers may know no-one in their building but visit regularly with friends ten miles away. Members of different social groups living in the same general area may have markedly different daily interaction patterns because they have different kinds of friends and a different past history of location in the city.

Knowledge of the individual interaction pattern will be of considerable importance in planning future cities. The pattern of daily travel is a key factor in both residence and commercial location. A family which has a large proportion of its trips in one direction, such as downtown, will be attracted that way, and only negative factors such as higher land costs and smaller lots will overcome the pressure. Stores prefer locations where the daily paths of many persons intersect so that trips made for one purpose will also serve for another.

In planning transportation needs, we need to know which are the critical kinds of movements to be eliminated. The journey-to-work is the most expensive urban movement because it clogs the highways at peak hours, yet there is some indication that many people don't mind this daily trip. Workers prefer to be isolated from their jobs, to separate their roles. When a husband is working he doesn't want to worry about the daily domestic crises, and when he gets home he wants to leave the worries of his job behind. Distance and traffic are thus a convenient as well as an inconvenient barrier.

It may be more important to reduce other kinds of daily travel: to bring schools closer to housing, to build them into apartment buildings or integrate them into residential blocks, or to make public recreation more accessible to more people. It's the children, after all, who don't have cars. Movement patterns like this help define a "community" which makes a good unit for the support of a school, a church, or a playground.

Most of the research on patterns of movement has come from transportation studies. The daily movement pattern of the entire metropolitan area is measured and related to the land use pattern of the city. Each urban activity creates a distinctive circulation pattern. For instance, a hospital serving the southwest part of the city contains 1,000 patients who come from that area, 2,000 employees who come from all over the city, and each day generates another 2,000 visitors. If another hospital is built in ten years, it should generate more traffic in the same manner. Thus traffic is related to land use. Once the pattern of movement in 1980 is estimated, its effect on the existing road and public transit system can be evaluated. Many present routes will be overloaded and will require replacement and enlargement.

But it gets complicated. New expressways change the pattern of accessibility in the city, leading to more rapid growth. Overcrowding of an expressway reduces speed, and the amount of use. These kinds of feedback make accurate predictions difficult.

We need much more information and better methods of working with the data before this kind of analysis of any behaviour pattern can be more than roughly useful. The central problem is deciding where prediction becomes control, and beyond that, where individuality loses its value. Should cities be consciously constructed? Or just left to grow? The answer, for this nation anyway, will probably lie somewhere in between.

BRIDGER, M. Keith and GREER-WOOTTEN, Bryn, "Landscape Components and Residential Urban Growth in Western Montreal Island," *Révue de Géographie de Montréal,* XIX, 1 and 2 (1965), pp. 75-90. An analysis of the attraction of various terrain characteristics for housing.

KAPLAN, Harold, *Urban Political Systems: A Functional Analysis of Metro Toronto* (New York: Columbia University Press, 1967). A political scientist analyses the day-to-day operations of Metro Toronto's Council. Don't be put off by the rather intimidating theoretical structure at the beginning.

LORIMER, James, *A Citizen's Guide to Urban Politics* (Toronto: James Lewis & Samuel, 1972). A disturbing examination of the way in which the "property industry" controls the development of our cities.

SPELT, Jacob, *Toronto* (Toronto: Collier-Macmillan, 1973). The best available comprehensive study of this city's growth and form.

TILLY, Charles, "Anthropology on the Town," *Habitat,* X, 1 (January-February, 1967), pp. 20-25. Approaches to the study of urban behaviour patterns.

WATSON, J. W., "Relict Geography in an Urban Community" in R. Mills and J. W. Watson (eds.), *Geographical Essays in Memory of Alan G. Ogilvie* (London: Thomas Nelson & Sons, 1959), pp. 110-143. A study of features remaining from the past in Halifax.

WOLFORTH, John R., *Residential Location and the Place of Work,* B.C. Geographical Series, No. 4 (Vancouver: Tantalus Research Ltd., 1965). Some of the complexities in daily movement patterns, as observed in Vancouver.

Central Mortgage and Housing Corporation

Toronto Star Syndicate

Ontario Ministry of Industry and Tourism

Ontario Ministry of Industry and Tourism

National Film Board of Canada

(following page) Central Mortgage and Housing Corporation

6 Patterns Within the City

Land Use

A city is an enormous and elaborate ant hill—the result of the apparently aimless and random workings of innumerable individuals, but exhibiting, in general, highly regular and predictable features. This pattern is the result of all the developmental decisions made in a city's history, with each one framed by the constraints of human behaviour and institutions discussed in the previous chapter.

The urbanologist looks at this pattern as the physical result of certain regular and repeated kinds of human activities. Certain things happen in certain areas of a city, and only there —the areas are therefore classified according to their land use. Elaborate typologies of land use have been developed. Commercial land, for instance, may be divided into retail, wholesale and office space; retail activities subdivided into food, hardware, and clothing; clothing, in turn, may include handbags or foundation garments.

The distribution of space in the gross categories of land use is quite stable from city to city. The majority of land is devoted to residential uses and the next largest use is streets and roads. The industry and commerce of the city, though a very visible component, actually occupies only a small part of the total land area.

Once an area is developed in a type of land use such as industrial or residential or recreational, the use generally continues for a long time. Considerable capital investment, not only in specific buildings but in streets and utilities and public buildings—schools and post offices—makes for stability; and other establishments of the same type move into the area, where facilities are known to exist and close linkages with associated activities can be established. Zoning legislation, too, tends to maintain the existing activities of the area.

Three main patterns of land use variations overlay each other: variations in intensity, variations in quality, and the less predictable variations due to major institutional locations. The most important of these is the pattern of intensity. As one goes away from the city centre the proportion of built-up land declines, the ratio of floor area to land area decreases, and the density of residents or employees per unit area declines. The major proportion of various land uses shifts toward less intensive activities like residence or recreation, and away from retail activities, high-rise apartments or office buildings, as the pressures of the market become less intense.

Within the broad land use categories the nature of use also changes. Near the city centre, residential areas consist of high-rise apartments or overcrowded tenements, walk-up apartments and boarding houses. Further out, single-family dwellings predominate and then slowly give way to strip developments along the highway, or half-acre estates at the edge of the city. Similarly, industry changes from five-story loft buildings with high employee density at the core of the city to extensive single-story highly automated factories with ample parking and landscaped grounds.

The regular changes in the intensity of land use are a product of the competition for accessibility to the urban area, and the growth pattern of the city. Cities exist for interaction —to let people and business establishments come in contact with one another. Stores must be within the closest possible touch of all potential customers. Lawyers, stockbrokers and banks must be near the other firms they deal with daily. City residents, all other things being equal, like to be as close as possible to stores, job opportunities and theatres.

The land use intensity patterns also demonstrate the sequence of technological and income changes expressed at different periods of development. Income increases have allowed us to spend greater sums on space, and the automobile has reduced the cost of extra distance travelled while increasing the space needed for parking. As a result, all kinds of land uses are declining in density over time. Most new stores are built as parts of shopping plazas. New manufacturing plants tend to be extremely spacious. Even new high-rise apartments or office buildings, despite their height, concentrate fewer people per square foot than structures of fifty years ago. Prestigious new downtown buildings incorporate plazas and plantings in their plans; the older buildings rise straight from the sidewalks. New buildings also employ more calculators and fewer clerks. Generally the buildings and the layout of the central city reflect the need for higher density at their period of development; those in the suburbs, the lower density requirements of today.

The second major land use pattern is the variations in the quality of the environment. Most major cities vary by sector. One sector will have a railroad track, a cluster of old factories, and housing with low-income tenants, approaching slum conditions. Another sector will be almost completely residential, of high quality, with open space—a ravine or a river—extensive parks, and perhaps institutional uses, like a university or hospital. These two ends of the scale indicate the regular sectoral variations in quality which exist and remain stable in most cities.

The sectors often follow transportation lines or topographic features which are attractive or unattractive to certain kinds of land uses. Wealthy families like to live along a ridge or ravine or shoreline, and dislike railroads and industry. The sectors also tend to be self-reinforcing. Once the initial patterns are identified, ambitious middle-class types shun the industrial working-class east end. Packing houses and auto wreckers

113

know they can never be accepted among the manicured lawns of an industrial park, nor can they overcome zoning restrictions in middle-class sectors given the incredible wrath of citizens who see a threat to their home values.

The third pattern is difficult to generalize. It is composed of the unique irregular nodes of activity which show up in most cities but in unpredictable locations, affecting the pattern of activities within the city almost as much as the original settlement site. A large institution like the University of British Columbia in Vancouver shapes the residential and commercial activities nearby. The Esquimalt naval base has a similar effect in Victoria as do the mineheads in Timmins and Sudbury. Sometimes another settlement centre alters the overall structure, as Waterloo and increasingly Galt do within the Kitchener metropolitan area. These secondary focal points, often highly specialized, create their own access patterns, modifying the whole journey-to-work flow, or the distribution of residential uses. Often they are the product of a single decision—the location of a university or an armed forces base—for some arbitrary reason several decades earlier.

The three types of land use variation, intensity, quality and institutional nodes, affect each of the traditional kinds of land use. Residential areas, the largest land use, will be treated at length in Chapter 7. The streets and roads network, the next largest use, was discussed in Chapter 5. Here we shall discuss three smaller but very significant uses: industrial areas, retail and service activities, and institutions.

The Economic Base

Most cities perform a specialized role within the national economy. A series of factories, a pulp mill or mine, a port or a railroad terminal—perhaps combinations of activities—stimulate the growth of the city and affect its land use pattern.

Sometimes the economic base is due to a single massive activity as in Arvida, Thetford Mines, or Sept Isles. The mine or port or army camp precedes the town and gets first choice of site. The town follows haphazardly, always dominated by the physical presence of the plant or the mine-head. The location of other activities is distorted by this single node which is the destination of all journeys-to-work, and by the necessity of developing in left-over areas.

In most cities, though, the port or the factories have emerged slowly over time. Old firms expand, new ones are begun or relocated. The location decisions are made over a long period of time according to the knowledge, the criteria and the competitive pressures of the time. Although in retrospect the locations of factories and office buildings seem uneconomical and shortsighted, at the time of their locations the alternatives were much more limited and the decisions much more logical.

Where should a brewery be located in Toronto in 1870? At that time a factory had to be accessible by workers on foot or by public transit, on a rail line since this was obviously the coming form of transportation, and with access to a steady supply of good water. Looking around a city of 50,000 the alternatives appeared pretty few. And, of course, no-one— planner or politician or industrialist—can see far into the urban future.

Unfortunately, the effects of early decisions tend to cumulate. Once a certain area in the city is identified as industrial, or a part of the waterfront is allocated to the port, the tendency is for new industrial or warehousing activities to locate nearby. A single factory can alienate a whole district. With time the industry and its associated activities, poor housing and heavy transport, march out in a sector to the edge of the city spreading noise, dirt and residential blight as they go. Regardless of site amenities or access advantages the quality of a sector has tremendous stability. There are very few examples of

115

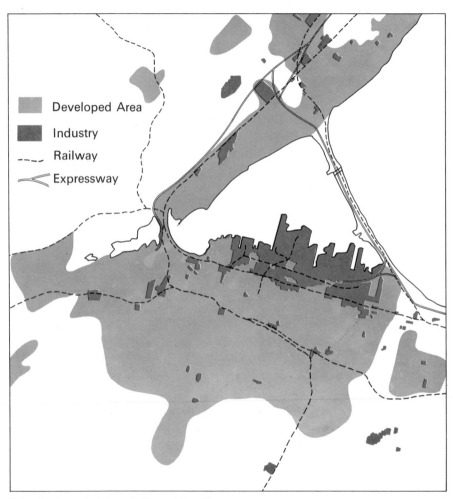

Developed Area
Industry
Railway
Expressway

6.1 Industrial Land Use: Hamilton

Based on data from Plate 5, *Economic Atlas of Ontario* (Toronto: University of Toronto Press, 1969), by courtesy of the Department of Treasury and Economics, Government of Ontario.

industrial land being reclaimed for more genteel activities, such as recreation or residential uses.

During the great burst of industrialization from 1870 to 1920 the railroads helped determine the location of those economic base activities which were not completely site-dependent. Access to a railroad was a necessity for a factory or port, so industry followed the tracks through the city. The railroads slashed across the city with little regard for the existing land use patterns, caring only for level routes without appreciable grade or sharp turns, and minimum construction costs. Local authorities were not about to let aesthetics get in the way of their city's survival.

Site or historical accident locate the railroad. The railroad locates the terminals and factories, which outline the structure of the town. Later additions to these complexes are determined by the earlier location patterns, even though in 1960 fresh water and railway access are not as important as parking space and an expressway entrance. The new firms need access to the old firms and the suppliers and services which already serve them. They need access to employees who live within the patterns set by earlier decisions. Each location decision affects all the decisions to follow.

But occasionally long-standing patterns are reversed. In some cities the railroad yards which despoiled the city core for a century are moving to the outskirts and so providing a source of low-density, one-owner land for redevelopment of the central city. Toronto, Montreal, Vancouver, Ottawa, Calgary and smaller centres are suddenly benefiting from the vacated railroad property which is attracting millions of dollars of new investment to replace the railroad tracks and yards.

The railroads' movement outward is in line with recent trends that show a deconcentration of basic activities. Increasingly, industrial activities are relocating to the city perimeter. Giant new port complexes like the Irving refinery in Saint John are being built away from the city core. Steel mills and oil refineries, too, are locating away from built-up areas—away from the restriction on sounds and smells and the presence of other land uses which create political pressures to restrict industrial expansion.

The automobile which transports the employees, the trucks which compete with the railroads, the telephones and telex networks which allow instant contact with other firms, all make decentralization possible. Congestion, the tendency to keep production lines on one level, the need for room to grow, provide the incentives for moving out from the city centre.

Retailing and Service

The commercial activities—retailing and service particularly—are the most visible of all the components of the urban landscape. The central commercial area of the city is the part we are most likely to have seen and to recognize, despite its relatively small land area. And the stores lining the arterial streets, the shopping centres, the little nodes of stores in older areas, are the most frequently passed and the best known parts of the cityscape. In some ways this is unfortunate, for the garish signs, the gaping parking lots, and the litter surrounding these activities are unpleasant aspects of a city. Practically any residential area looks more attractive than its shopping facilities.

The screaming signs and the concentration of stores in the city's most frequented areas both result from the desperate struggle of commercial enterprises to keep alive. The turnover in such activities is tremendous—up to twenty-five per cent of the stores now in business will have gone broke, or moved, or changed ownership within the next year. Hence, appropriate location is a matter of great concern to stores. The owner weighs off several different factors, with priorities determined

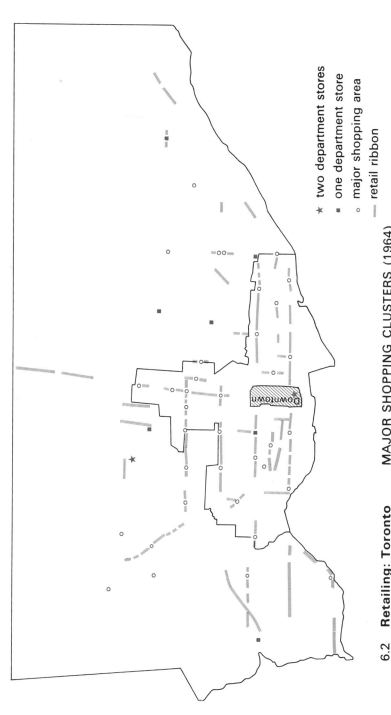

legend:
★ two department stores
■ one department store
○ major shopping area
▨ retail ribbon

Downtown

6.2 Retailing: Toronto   MAJOR SHOPPING CLUSTERS (1964)

Based on data from James W. Simmons, *Toronto's Changing Retail Complex* (Chicago: University of Chicago, Department of Geography, Research Paper No. 104, 1966).

by the type of store he runs: automobile or pedestrian traffic, the kind of customer (income, sex, etc.), the amount and purpose of the traffic, the kinds of neighbouring stores, and, of course, the cost of land or rent. These factors restrict location fairly severely. Given the existing pattern of store locations and the circulation pattern of a city it is possible to specify the two or three most likely locations for any activity.

The variety of activities and their grouping and distribution in space are remarkably constant from city to city. Some kinds of stores tend to cluster together in nodes or shopping centres which serve the surrounding neighbourhoods of the urban area—much as market towns serve the nearby countryside. A range of these centres of different sizes exists in each city. The largest and most fully equipped shopping area is downtown, called the central business district (CBD) by planners, which serves the entire city and its trade area. Other small centres within the city provide less unusual and more widely used goods to individual sections of the city. Within the service area of these smaller centres, in turn, will be half a dozen even smaller clusters which serve the immediate neighbourhoods.

The range of sizes of centres and the variety of facilities at each one will depend on the size of the city. Toronto has a very large downtown shopping area with two large department stores, but several suburban shopping plazas also have two major department stores and challenge the downtown centre in some ways. Another dozen or so centres in the metropolitan area have department stores—forming the next level—and below them are the innumerable community centres with a large supermarket, a dime store, or a discount store and other stores. Below that is the grocery store, drugstore, dry cleaners combination—and at the lowest, most ubiquitous level, the corner variety store: five levels in all. Yorkton or Trenton, on the other hand, may contain only the lower three levels.

These centres locate where they are most central to the population they serve and most accessible to it. Within the centre they jostle each other into some form of order according to their ability to make use of and pay for access to customers. The corner location by the bus stop is always the best, and the spur-of-the-moment items are sold there, in the cigar stores and candy stores. The shopping stores with clothes, shoes, and so on, will be nearby. They must cluster close to one another because shoppers like to compare goods and prices from different stores, but are not willing to go out of their way to do so. These kinds of stores will not be found in the smaller centres where the pedestrian traffic is too low.

In the past these shopping areas have emerged gradually, growing in competition with other centres nearby, and adjusting internally as old stores went broke and new stores came in. As the centre grew, stores grew; certain activities prospered while others withdrew. The last twenty years have witnessed a new phenomenon, the planned shopping plaza, a complete shopping centre planned and erected all at once to serve a specific area and a specific number of customers. Now plazas are established at the furthest edges of the city long before an area is completely built up. They dominate the retailing in those parts of the city built in the last fifteen years, yet they pose some difficult problems for orderly urban growth because of their inflexibility.

All aspects of such a plaza—the physical plant, the number, size and layout of stores, the parking spaces, as well as the type of retail activities—are geared to a specific size of centre, and thus to a specific location. A centre cannot grow or change level by adding new stores. If no new plaza is built nearby, the customer in the trade area is at the mercy of the businessmen of the single plaza, who face little nearby competition since few plazas contain duplicate kinds of stores. On the other hand if a new—and especially a larger—plaza is constructed, the merchants in the original plaza are faced with instant, overwhelming competition. Shoppers will flock to the larger centre with the bigger department store. At the losing plaza stores go out of business and vacancy signs go up; the plaza assumes that seedy run-down look and attracts only marginally successful stores. Meanwhile traffic and zoning problems for the community have doubled.

Thus the very size of the plazas leads to planning problems although their integrated design and off-street parking offer real advantages. In practice, most of the disputes about the zoning of such activities are really fronts for the two opposing entrepreneurs—those who own the existing plaza, and those who wish to invade with a new one. Arguments about who will make the profit are clothed with planning principles, while planning principles are ignored in the face of political and economic realities. The influence of the downtown merchants, the attempts of politicians to increase a city's assessment, or the interest of a large department store chain have far more influence than the city planner.

The forgotten man in these hassles is usually the customer. His preferences for strong competition and easily accessible facilities are seldom expressed in the arguments about shopping plaza sizes and locations. As a result the customer seeks the variety he desires by visiting several plazas, refusing to be tied to the nearest one. Increasingly, competition is no longer among stores but among plazas.

In spite of the automobile and the trend to decentralization, the central business district of the city maintains formidable concentrations of employment and public investment. The personal contact—for business or pleasure—is still a necessary element, and the most important function of urban places. The downtown area still characterizes a city, providing the milieu for a swinging population; indicating the local political preference for assessment or parks; generating an aura of growth, or tinging the whole city with the faint smell of decay.

The central business district is a complex and fascinating area, particularly as a city grows beyond the size of two or three hundred thousand. It covers only a small area, but has a number of the oldest and newest buildings in the city, and includes half a dozen diverse and colorful sub-areas within walking distance. Generally, it is easy to identify the core—the cluster of specialized shopping activities which gradually grades off in all directions into specialized clusters of different activities. The sub-areas outside the core depend not on the shopping habits of the whole city, but on access to certain types of potential customers: stockbrokers, wealthy women, or the down-and-out.

Often there is a secondary shopping node—located toward the wealthy section of town at the expanding edge of the CBD—where well-to-do shoppers buy fashion items in smaller, more exclusive shops: Toronto's Bloor Street, Montreal's Sherbrooke Street, Vancouver's Georgia Street. The financial centre —the cluster of banks, trust companies and brokers—is usually at the other end of the central area. These complexes establish themselves early and become well-nigh immovable because of the tremendous investments in high-rise offices and the intricate net of communications. Still another area includes the expanding modern office buildings where image-conscious companies locate their headquarters: advertising agencies, successful lawyers and physicians, and the newest, most expensive hotels.

In another section, frequently down towards the railroad and bus stations and slums, the CBD is decaying. Cheap hotels, dingy restaurants, pool rooms, pawnshops—perhaps skid row in the larger cities—continue to survive, waiting until the city gets around to carrying out its urban renewal plan.

The cheap bars, the innumerable offices, and the witty boutiques—are all necessary to a large city, but their varied requirements are complex and difficult to plan. It is difficult to envisage any kind of planned or designed area which would have the diversity, the flexibility of the areas which already exist. Frequently the city tends to gestures on the grand scale: the enormous avenue—6 or 8 lanes—lined with monumental buildings, or a massive city hall in the heart of what is in essence, an extremely compact, intimate group of establishments. But these only mar the purposeful concentration that has been attained. Even in our largest cities, despite the enormous amounts of employment and merchandising involved, central business districts are seldom more than a mile across, and probably occupy less than 3 per cent of the total land area of the city.

Public and Institutional

The regularities in the distribution of retail and service activities are determined by the operation of the marketplace. In the search for profits, stores adjust their location, the kind of goods they sell, and their size to the needs of their customers. By contrast, a much larger part of the urban landscape—the public and institutional activities—is formed only indirectly by market demands. Politicians and technicians locate schools, parks and expressways according to quite different criteria.

Public facilities are often part of a network so that the existing system determines where new elements must go. A new water main or sewage plant, a new high school, must fit into the rest of the system. Instead of seeking out competition, public facilities avoid it. *This* is your school; you will pick up post office parcels *here; Fire Station Number 3* will answer your call.

The location of public facilities in turn is often a powerful determinant of other land uses. The extensions of sewers, waterlines or expressways accelerate or constrain private development. But, more directly, the public economy is a significant part of the city itself, providing employment for up to 20 per cent of the workers and occupying 30 to 40 per cent of the land (including streets). Hence, public sector decisions can play a large part in the image and the workings of the city.

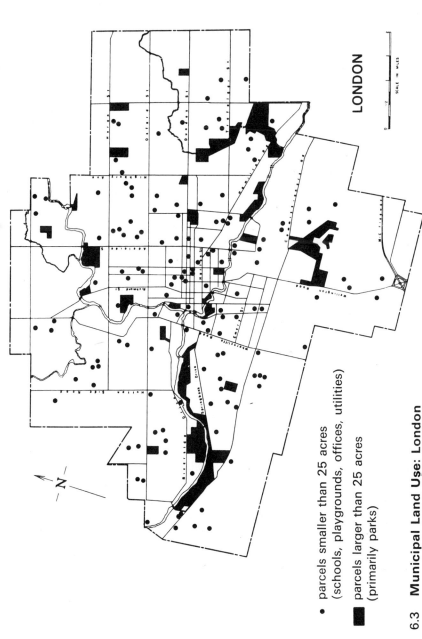

- parcels smaller than 25 acres
  (schools, playgrounds, offices, utilities)

■ parcels larger than 25 acres
  (primarily parks)

LONDON

SCALE IN MILES

6.3 Municipal Land Use: London

Victor Huebert, *Public Land-Use in London Ontario*, unpublished M.A. thesis, University of Western Ontario (London, Ontario: 1967), Reproduced by permission of the author.

The trouble is that many of the public decisions are unpredictable. In Metro Toronto an arbitrary decision by the province ordained that there be six boroughs (before there were twelve; a Royal Commission suggested four). Each borough is now planning a civic centre with commercial and public utilities located in the centre of its territory. Traffic and employment characteristics will be changed—unless, of course, the province changes its mind.

Aside from the regularities guaranteed by the non-competitive network of services, and in the absence of the clear-cut economic criteria of commercial development, it is difficult to determine the amount of demand for a park, or the priority that a park should have over a new police station, or better welfare facilities, or a raise for city council members. The endless tedious debate by the municipal council at budget time is part of its method of evaluating needs and priorities, although the requirements of the public are sometimes distorted by the personal prejudices of politicians, or a single vivid incident, a tragic traffic death, or a human interest eviction, or an accusation of graft. The public budget is generally viewed through the eyes of a small-time businessman, and the public itself becomes aroused only when a fire in a school, or a rape in broad daylight focuses attention on a particular problem.

Larger, more unusual items—a city hall, a major park, a centennial arena or urban renewal project—are often extremely contentious problems in terms of cost and of location, and municipal authorities may argue them for years. All sorts of lobbies are mobilized: ratepayers from one ward want an arena; those from another oppose a garbage dump. Senior citizens prefer a centennial home for the aged to a centennial skating rink. Certain members of the city council are opposed to anything the mayor wants. The planning board refuses to accept any of the suggested projects.

As a result, the public part of the landscape may be spectacularly varied. Favourable financial conditions, a flash of insight by an influential politician, and a lot of luck may lead to a Toronto City Hall, or an Expo. More likely the city will end up with no facility at all, or a succession of makeshift establishments.

All levels of government contribute to urban public facilities. Every downtown has its post office or federal building. Few are visual assets, although some of the airports built by the Department of Transport are more successful, like Toronto's or Edmonton's.

Provincial governments provide much of the funds for schools, universities, and hospitals, but tend to transfer control of spending to local authorities. The result seems to be greater variance in the style and effectiveness of such institutions. To a greater extent than the federal buildings they reflect the regional culture.

The works of the local government are the best indicators of the city's character. Out of the haggling of civic politicians have emerged some fascinating and distinctive activities: public open places—the squares in central Montreal; various kinds of City Halls; and the parks—formal or informal, numerous or scattered. All these indicate how citizens respond to their physical environment and to their history.

The public open places within the city generate a variety of activities and local traditions: skating at Toronto's City Hall, sexual skirmishing along the promenade by the Chateau in Quebec City; canoeing on Ottawa's canal; kite-flying off Calgary's north hill by the Jubilee Auditorium.

Considering the impact of public decisions, and their apparent freedom from the usual economic constraints, one could wish for a little more imagination in their making. However, one soon realizes that these decisions, too, are products of many forces: they are the result of the composition of a governing body, and that governing body itself is the reflection of a whole culture's desires.

BEAUREGARD, Ludger (ed.), *Montreal Field Guide* (Montreal: Presses de l'Université de Montréal, 1972). A series of articles summarize the Montreal landscape and its evolution.

BOAL, F. W. and JOHNSON, D. B., "The Functions of Retail and Service Establishments on Commercial Ribbons," *Canadian Geographer,* IX, 3 (1965), pp. 154-169. This study stresses the linkages among stores: how customers move from one to another.

BOURNE, Larry S., *Private Redevelopment of the Central City: Spatial Processes of Structural Change in the City of Toronto* (Chicago: University of Chicago, Department of Geography, Research Paper No. 112, 1967). How activities and land uses replace one another.

BOURNE, L. S., MacKINNON, R. D., and SIMMONS, J. W. (eds.), *The Form of Cities in Central Canada: Selected Papers* (Toronto: University of Toronto, Department of Geography, Research Paper No. 11, 1973). A series of papers describing spatial patterns and behaviour within cities in Ontario and Quebec.

DEPARTMENT OF DEFENSE, EMERGENCY MEASURES ORGANIZATION, *Urban Analysis Maps* (Ottawa: Department of Energy, Mines and Resources, Surveys and Mapping Branch). A series of thirty-two maps describe the setting and land use of Vancouver in great detail. A few maps are also available for Toronto.

FORWARD, Charles N., *Waterfront Land Use in Metropolitan Vancouver, British Columbia,* Geographical Paper No. 41, Geographical Branch, Department of Energy, Mines and Resources (Ottawa: Queen's Printer, 1968). Examines the use of the Vancouver shoreline.

Habitat. A quarterly magazine published by Central Mortgage and Housing Corporation and distributed free. It is concerned with development and quality of the Canadian urban environment.

SIMMONS, James W., *Toronto's Changing Retail Complex* (Chicago: University of Chicago, Department of Geography, Research Paper No. 104, 1966). Examines the distribution of retail and service facilities in the metropolitan area.

7 People

The Patterns of Residence

The city, above all else, is a place where people live. The predominant urban land use is residential, and it is the character of the residents that gives different cities and different parts of the cities much of their individuality. All the physical characteristics—setting, street plan, architecture—can be overcome, transformed, or submerged by the sheer colour or lack of it of the inhabitants.

In central Toronto, the straight, rigid files of streets and the tall, gloomy, Victorian-fronted buildings have been submerged by the Sicilian, Portuguese and Peloponnesian immigrants perched on their elaborately carved stoops, grouping and reforming on their sidewalks, leaning volubly out of their narrow windows. At the other extreme, think of the beautiful, crescented woodland suburbs, originally laid out with loving, tree-conscious care and now covered with houses whose massive front doors, vacant lawns, and heavily-draped windows advertise the possessive gloom of their owners.

What is fascinating about the urban social landscape is the consistency with which different social groups sort themselves out into regular patterns. The pressures of family size and pocketbook, coupled with the historical accident of initial location, produce amazingly homogeneous neighbourhoods, grouped according to age, income, and ethnic background.

Moreover, these communities often remain stable for long periods of time, although change, if it does take place, may relocate the population of an entire sector almost at once. Within ten years the Italian community of Toronto, now some 300,000 strong, has carved out a huge area for itself. But on

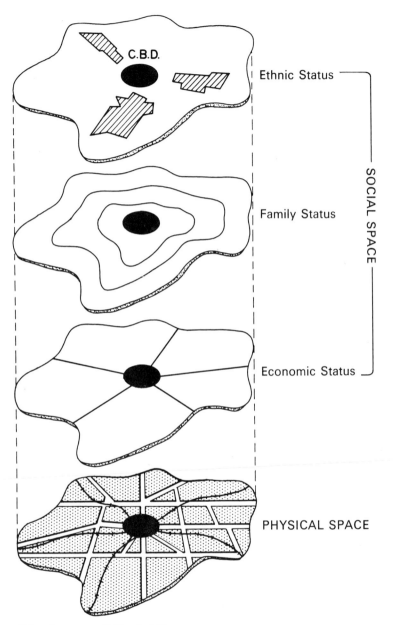

7.1 Layers of Social Space

Robert A. Murdie, *Factorial Ecology of Metropolitan Toronto, 1951-1961* (Chicago: University of Chicago, Department of Geography, Research Paper No. 116, 1969, p. 9). Reproduced by permission of the author.

the other side of town, the Anglo-Saxon working-class areas have been occupied by the same kind of people for a hundred years. In Montreal, most of the Jewish community has removed itself from the cramped streets near Boulevard St. Laurent to Côte St. Luc and the other spacious suburbs north and west of Mont Royal, but the traditional English enclaves of Westmount and Pointe Claire continue to survive.

Some of the changes are gradual and predictable, such as the continuing move to the suburbs as the city grows, and the outward expansion of higher income areas. Others, such as the moves by ethnic communities mentioned above, or the rapid decay of a once fashionable area, take place rapidly and often without warning.

Rings of Demographic Characteristics

The important demographic characteristics are age, marital and family status, and their spatial distribution produces the same regular pattern in most cities, obscured only by local topographical features. The pattern is the same set of rings that shows in studies of a city's growth, with regular variations in these characteristics as one moves outward from the city centre.

At the core of the city are the high-density housing areas: boarding houses, flats, and high-rise apartments. These are occupied by young single men and women, the newly married, or the aged who have always lived there or have moved into lodgings or small apartments upon retirement or widowhood.

Within this broad area are a number of smaller communities—better developed and more visible in large cities. The elderly tend to locate together near the centre of the city, choosing environments according to their incomes. A famous sociological study describes the "Gold Coast and the Slum"—a part of the central city that includes within one or two blocks some of the richest and poorest inhabitants of the city. In the larger cities some of the most exclusive downtown apartments are filled with elderly ladies, accompanied by paid companions and small dogs. To pass for inspection in front of the residents of such retirement apartments or hotels is a humbling experience; but probably more disturbing is to pass among the aged eking out pensions in cheap boarding houses and skid row areas. Many of the residents found among the bars and flophouses and pawnshops of skid row are pensioners forced to live there because it is cheap.

Sociologically, the younger occupants of the high-rise apartments—the swinging cliff dwellers—are a recent and fascinating phenomenon. They are a direct result of affluence and the non-family household; a generation ago they would all have lived with their parents. Although the buildings are filled with young, single men and women, entirely free and on their own, there is little intermingling socially among the inhabitants of the same building. One soon realizes that the primary demands of these people are privacy and independence. They don't want to know who their neighbours are or what they do, and they don't want their neighbours to know what *they* are doing.

Physically the buildings and the apartments are almost all alike. There may be a slightly different décor in the lobby, or a pretentious name like "El Camaro" over the door, but the distribution of apartments, their size and layout are identical. If one doesn't suit there are a dozen similar at the same rents, and you may swap a sauna for underground parking. Their availability plus the rather temporary nature of many of the households which inhabit them lead to very high mobility rates—up to 50 per cent a year. They are inhabited by college students, working girls, or newlyweds looking for a house. In larger cities the high transient rate leads to further sorting out. Certain apartments cater to the retired; others are for airline stewardesses, or college professors.

132

From bohemians to hippies to freaks—on the margin between the cheap older housing of the central core and the twentieth-century affluence of the high-rise areas is a region devoted to unconventional life-styles—speed freaks, communes, and head shops. This area is an essential part of the city; small towns have no room or tolerance for such areas.

Five years later probably both the hippies and the swingers will find themselves in the suburbs, the antithetical environment. Gone is the isolation, the independence, the tolerance of the central city. Suburban residents are facing the long-run problems of life: earning a living, raising a family, surviving in a complex self-critical middle-class culture. There are overwhelming pressures to meet neighbours, join institutions, and daily reaffirm one's belief in the values of the community. Neighbours introduce themselves; housewives have regular communal coffee breaks; and husbands gather in knots at the fence corners to share beer and success stories.

These communities in the outermost urban ring are extremely homogeneous in their life cycle stage. The number and ages of children in each block, almost in each home, are highly predictable. The waves of city growth generate a series of these demographic ripples which continue outward for years and years. Planned in 1952, constructed in 1953, Bienvenue Acres came to life in 1954. Most of the families moving in had one child and another on the way. By 1960 most of the child-bearing had ceased, and the wave had hit the local public school (which was, inevitably, unprepared). Now a new high school is being built; fathers, mortgaged to the hilt by 1953 wage levels, are feeling affluent: adding a garage, finishing the basement, cluttering the house with plastic awnings, expensive shrubs, lawn decorations, fancy aluminum doors. Those who are really making it move away to a better district.

Between the suburbs and the city centre lie the rings of earlier development—other homogeneous communities at other stages of their life cycle. In the older areas, the suburbs of

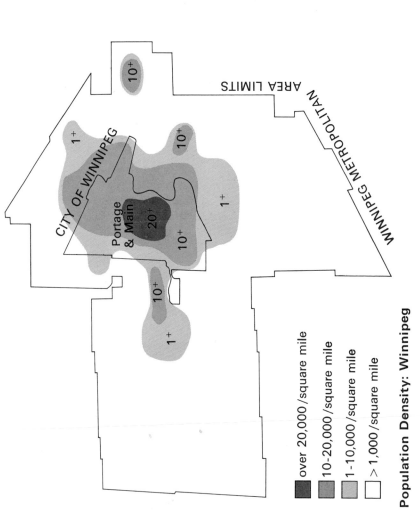

7.2 **Population Density: Winnipeg**

over 20,000 /square mile

10-20,000 /square mile

1-10,000 /square mile

> 1,000 /square mile

twenty or thirty years ago, the families are growing up; the whole neighbourhood hovers on the brink of change. In a rapidly growing city general transformations take place at this stage: walk-up apartment buildings in the vacant lots near the bus stops, additions to the houses for extra boarders, expansion of commercial activities. If the growth of the city has slowed down, the area may stabilize instead into what planners picture as the perfect urban environment: a mature suburb, with all public facilities established and paid off, and a good mix of families at all stages in the life cycle. Increasingly, though, it seems that the speed of growth and the tendency to design and segregate housing for specific age groups are attacking this planners' dream.

The distribution of the sexes differs throughout the city and at different times of day. Elderly widows and younger working women live in apartments and rooming houses in the high-income sectors of the city. They pay premium prices for neighbourhoods which are less threatening and better served by public transportation. The distribution of daytime population includes the ring of suburban housewives who live in a nine to five female culture. Transportation services, shopping facilities, and institutions recognize these subtle patterns.

The basic demographic variation outward from the city centre is typical of all income levels. The demographic character of the city centre—that apparently anomalous but logical mixture of the young and private, and the old and lonely—does not vary from the creaking rooming house to the carpeted high-rise; nor does the family pattern of the unserviced do-it-yourself tarpaper subdivision vary from that of the district of split-level two-car garages. The only possible exception is the ethnic ghetto, where newcomers to Canada concentrate in tight communities near the city centre. Since immigrants are predominantly young, often with children, they may distort the expected demographic pattern.

Wedges of Social Class

Regular patterns of social class overlay the demographic pattern. Social class is an amalgam of the closely related factors of income, education, and occupation. The pattern it produces may vary in detail from city to city, but in most cases it subdivides the demographic rings into wedge-shaped sectors. For example, the high-income part of the city generally extends in one sector of the city from downtown right out to the suburbs.

Every small town, as every small-towner knows, has its right and wrong side of the tracks; but many city-dwellers may not consciously realize the extent to which these patterns continue as the city grows in size. The income sectors move ever outward in steadily widening wedges. The income characteristics of Toronto's Rosedale, for example, extend right on out along Bayview Avenue to the quarter-million dollar suburban estates along the Bridle Path. Similarly, low-income sectors, comprised of high-density slums near the core, follow the railroad out to cheap, single-family bungalows built on the bleak flatlands of the perimeter.

With few exceptions these patterns are consistent for most cities, and absorb many smaller patterns within them. Income, for example, tends to vary not only sectorally, but with distance from the city centre, and reflects the relations between income and demographic characteristics. Income is lowest for those at either end of the productive period, the young and the old at the city centre, and highest for the middle-aged inhabitants of the older suburbs.

The class structure of even the smallest city is infinitely subtle and complex. Within the general ordering from lower to higher there are parallel routes, dead end branches, and peculiar exceptions and contradictions. Each of the major ethnic groups has its own hierarchy and lower-ranking members of

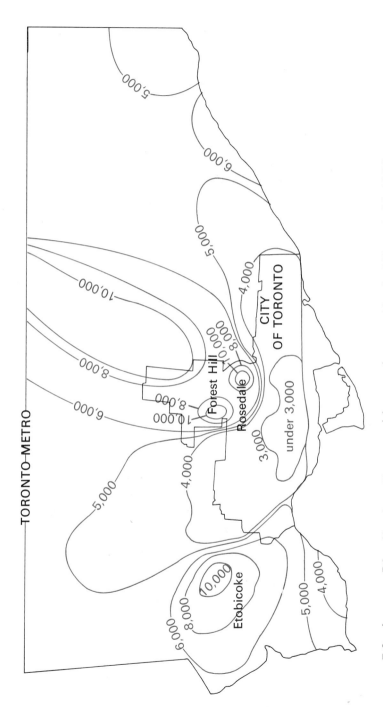

7.3 **Income Distribution: Toronto** (*Average Income, Head of Household, 1961*)
Data obtained from Statistics Canada, *Census of Canada, 1961.*

some groups claim superiority over the leaders of lesser groups. Intellectual and professional people have their own standards as well.

Because Canada is a nation of immigrants, family ancestry counts in only the limited number of cities where two or three generations have succeeded their successful merchant forebears. The older cities of Quebec and the Loyalist cities like Kingston and Fredericton have developed this kind of tradition, but social achievement for the most part is due to a combination of financial success, ethnic origin, and cultural pretensions.

A key indicator of class aspiration is the neighbourhood of residence. At the upper end of the scale the possible locations of each type are reduced to very few, leading to incredible concentrations of financial and political power within small areas. The residential neighbourhood of Rosedale, for instance, contains a major proportion of who's who in Toronto. Forest Hill is another acceptable area but tends to be a bit more *nouveau*. In Montreal the communities of Westmount and Outremont shelter the leaders of the English and French communities respectively. In smaller cities, like London or Regina or Sherbrooke, all the élite are concentrated within a few blocks.

The general pattern includes the really top people, who tend to withdraw to estates around the edges of the city; the farther and larger the estate, the greater the success. (The company president lives out in the urban fringe beyond Metro Toronto, but the board chairman has withdrawn all the way to the Bahamas.) The next level of those who have made it is concentrated in one or two proper residential districts, well known throughout the city, like Rockcliffe or Winnipeg's Tuxedo. At the next jump down, the upper middle class, the alternatives really widen. One must specialize within the income group. In Vancouver, for instance, you can rent a $500 per month apartment overlooking English Bay, or buy an architect-designed aerie on the North Shore, or a commodious older home on the fringe of Shaughnessy Heights.

Below this level, people live where they can first, afford, and second, obtain, the kind of housing they need. If the city is growing, like Calgary and Edmonton, old housing near the city centre is rapidly priced out of reach, and suburbia is the only viable choice. In non-growing towns like Saint John or Timmins where wages are rising even more slowly than the price of housing, there may well be no alternative to an older frame house in the city centre. Working-class families are particularly dependent on kinship contacts, particularly among mothers and daughters, but also with more distant relatives. These relationships can be maintained if housing is available near the old neighbourhood, but if the rate of growth forces children to move far away to a suburban neighbourhood, family life may undergo considerable stress.

The low-income groups, those on welfare or pensions, the disabled and the alcoholics, drift wherever they can afford to go. They occupy the residual areas that no one else wants. An urban renewal programme, or a new expressway or office building, will push them on to another neighbourhood without effective protest. They have few possessions, few institutions to serve them, and use facilities that require little capital investment.

The Ethnic and Religious Clusters

Superimposed on the demographic and social class patterns are the ethnic and religious variables which provide the third major dimension of urban social variation. Like the dimension of social class, these ethnic-religious concentrations tend to form sectoral rather than ring patterns. Where the ethnic minority is small, less than 20% of the population, it

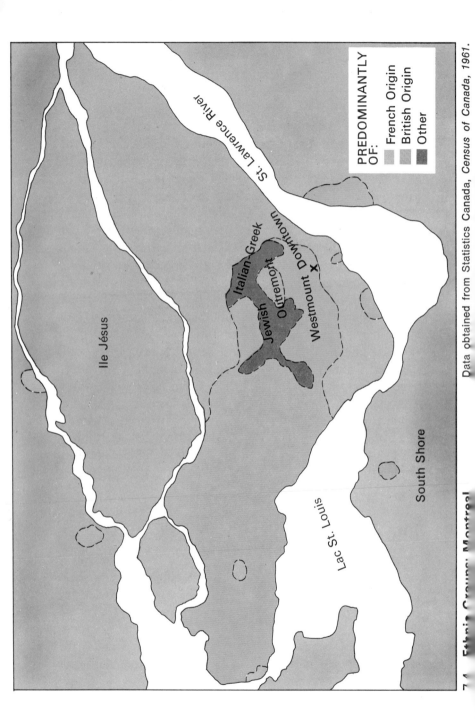

7.4 Ethnic Groups: Montreal

Data obtained from Statistics Canada, *Census of Canada, 1961.*

PREDOMINANTLY OF:
- French Origin
- British Origin
- Other

St. Lawrence River

Ile Jésus

Italian-Greek
Jewish
Outremont
Downtown
Westmount
X

Lac St. Louis

South Shore

may group in a single cluster—a small area overlaying the social class and demographic patterns. For a larger minority, the node expands in the familiar wedge-shaped pattern towards the edge of the city.

The ethnic-religious variations are particularly significant in Canadian cities for two reasons. The first, of course, is the two-nation origin of the country that splits Montreal and Winnipeg, for example, into such obviously different sections that the names of their respective minority areas—Westmount and St. Boniface—have become nationally famous. In Montreal the clearly defined English-speaking area is west from Mont Royal, and the French-speaking area solidly to the east. In Winnipeg the old French-speaking community located on the east side of the Red River has expanded to the east and south while being enveloped by the growth of the city itself.

But also of great significance is the wave of recent immigration. Nearly all these newcomers settle in urban surroundings, and their presence results, as in Toronto, in just as startlingly visible divisions between English and Italian as the French-English split in Montreal. The Italians dominate a large sector of the city, west from Bathurst to the Humber River along the community's main artery, College Street. The store signs, advertisements, and owners' names in this section are solidly and visibly Italian for blocks. Throughout the city the signs at large construction projects and in many industrial plants are in English and Italian. Montreal is the second largest French-speaking city in the world, and Toronto's Little Italy is one of the dozen largest Italian cities.

Other Canadian cities, particularly those in the west, display the culture of Germans, Chinese, Ukrainians, and others. Many of these concentrations of national or cultural groups have been in existence as long as the city itself. They have contributed to the growth of the city at each stage in its development. The continuous influx of immigration since World War II has added new groups and new residents to areas already established. Most Canadian metropolitan areas now have three or more readily identifiable ethnic areas, indicating a concentration of over 10,000 or so persons of a given background within the city.

The threshold of a community's visibility varies with both the ethnic group and the city size. Groups such as the Chinese, or southern Europeans like Italians, Portuguese and Greeks, stay close together and initiate highly visible activities—food stores, restaurants, curio shops. Others, such as the British, the Germans and the Dutch disperse rapidly to the suburbs. The larger the city, the larger an ethnic community must be to be visible. Toronto's two million people hide even such colorful groups as the 10,000 (India) Indians and 30,000 Maltese. In a city of 10,000, however, even one imported British plant manager and his family make an impact.

Among the most visible communities are the Chinese districts in Toronto and Vancouver. In each case the community is beginning to disperse because it occupies the fringe of highly valuable downtown commercial areas—land which is valuable for other uses, and unattractive to the increasingly middle-class Chinese residents. The change shows itself in two ways. First, there is an increasing commercialization of cultural differences, as only the enterprises capitalizing on the ethnic group's unique flavour and central city position survive—the highly visible restaurants and gift shops. Secondly, the process of acculturation is in a considerably advanced state—the "Chinese" waitresses and shop girls speak pure Canadian despite the slits in the sides of their skirts. Yet the very fact of the ability of such older ethnic communities to maintain, indeed, to capitalize on, their differences indicates that the present ethnic concentrations will be contributing their individuality to the city's diversity for a long time to come.

More residential and extremely cohesive are the Jewish communities, which stay together as the whole group relocates from one neighbourhood to another. Toronto's Bathurst Street cuts across the entire range of social classes and life stages. It began in the old near-slum core around Kensington Market and moved northward through the rich older suburb of Forest Hill to the lower-middle-class subdivisions and high-rise apartments of Downsview. Jewish families shift back and forth along this artery, adjusting their housing to their family needs and to their economic success, but always remaining part of the community.

Hungarians, Greeks, Portuguese, and West Indians also cluster in different parts of the cities, often near each other, sometimes following in the wake of other upwardly mobile groups, but invariably concentrated and easily identified. Corner groceries, restaurants and coffee shops with placards in the old country language are the first signs. The Acropolis restaurant, the Budapest Bakery, the Napoli grocery store and the Algarve fish market add colour and a variety of sounds, smells and tastes to many Canadian cities, where thirty years ago a fish and chip shop was the height of specialty eating.

Later, as the ethnic community grows, a variety of services—lawyers, realtors, driving schools, even radio programmes—emerge to serve the population. Institutions, churches, clubs and athletic teams follow. The earliest migrants begin to move out of the poorer housing of the initial settlement, but they continue to have strong ties to the stores and organizations of the ethnic core. If immigration continues, the core is continually replenished with new arrivals.

In a curious contradiction, the largest groups of recent immigrants to Canada are the most totally assimilated. The British, the German, the Dutch are dispersed throughout the metropolitan area. Occasionally when you enter a store the copies of *Der Spiegel* or the Dutch chocolate and cigars identify the origin of the owner, but these groups, middle-class and white collar to a great extent, competent in English and coming from cultures similar in many ways to the basic Canadian mix, have their greatest cultural impact in the gradual long-run modification of "Canadian" customs, mostly by widening the range of choice in foodstuffs, in liquor laws, in sports or entertainments.

Thus, on one hand distinct ethnic communities with their own commercial centres and institutions are emerging, while in other ways, and for other groups, assimilation, at least as far as visibility is concerned, is almost complete. The largest ethnic and cultural group remains the least visible or least obvious, because its influence is so pervasive. The Anglo-Saxon Protestant middle-class community centred around the Anglican and United Churches remains, as John Porter has shown, the dominant force in the political and social institutions of the country. It provides political leaders at all levels, the academic élite, the civil service, and controls the main financial institutions of the country.

In Quebec, a French-Canadian élite shares some areas of this influence, being particularly dominant in religion, academics, politics and the provincial civil service. Aside from Montreal with its sizeable British (18%) and non-English, non-French (15%) stock, the cities of Quebec are almost completely homogeneous in ethnic origin. In-migrants come from surrounding rural areas, rather than from other provinces or other countries.

In Canada, as in the United States, the melting pot melts only so far. The Anglo-Saxons, the Jews, the French Canadians, the Eastern and Southern Europeans, will be distinct and visible elements in Canadian urban life for some time to come. The challenge to politicians and planners will be to provide a place for each group without bitterness, injustice or prejudice. This is often difficult when ethnic origins are closely linked with economic levels, and access to political power is made difficult by outdated institutions and jealous politicians. The use of larger units of representation and the careful selection of ward boundaries keep control in the hands of older immigrant groups and middle-class voters.

144

How Patterns of Residence Change

The various kinds of neighbourhoods—the ghettos, the exclusive suburbs, the slums—do not emerge by chance. People move to these areas by their own choice, but they act within a narrow set of constraints. They seek a new home which will best satisfy their housing needs within the limits set by income and accessibility and their limited knowledge of housing opportunities. As in the process of development, discussed earlier, the environment imposes powerful constraints on the decision makers.

Each year one family in five changes its residence. Even without physical change—demolition and construction—cities are continually transformed as the population grows, ages and relocates. Although, for the most part, each outgoing family is replaced by another quite similar to it, the potential does exist, and occasionally is realized, for very rapid alteration in the character of a neighbourhood. Within ten years 70% to 80% of the housing in any area could be occupied by a different ethnic or income group, without any element of flight on the part of the original occupants, but simply through normal replacement.

This continuous movement permits the rapid expansion of the Italian sector in Toronto, the rapid filling up of a new apartment in Vancouver or the maintenance of a Montreal slum for several decades. It all depends on whether or not the same kind of people move in as moved out.

By and large, most areas are remarkably stable, attracting the same kind of residents for many decades. The intimate network of social contacts and the neighbourhood organizations and facilities tend to maintain the pattern. Families move primarily to adjust housing itself. They are satisfied with the character and location of the neighbourhood, but they need an extra bedroom or they hear of a "nicer" place, or they want to

145

own instead of renting. If they can satisfy their housing demands, they will often relocate nearby, within a few blocks.

The great bulk of moves are made between the ages of sixteen and thirty—leaving home, getting a job, marriage, children—and each stage requires a new residence. This selection shapes the social structure of the city. Generally, three factors are involved: the needs of the household, the housing supply, and the information linking demand and supply.

The family's requirements must be categorized. They are partly physical: four children and two dogs require a certain amount of room; partly cultural: "all our friends have built-in garbage-disposal units" or "Betty says there's only one decent school in the whole city"; and partly economic: "we can't carry payments of more than $200 per month".

On the supply side the decision is affected, of course, by the availability of different kinds of housing. What is the variety at a given price: apartments, townhouses, old mansions, new architect-designed boxes? Here the developer's decisions and the city's growth rate play important roles. In city X there are currently available twenty-three houses with payments less than $200, five of which have at least three bedrooms, and all of them in the same neighbourhood. From this selection the family chooses one to satisfy its requirements.

But this is the theoretical ideal; demand and supply are never defined so neatly in the real world. Households find it difficult to express exactly what they want. Indeed, they are often willing to trade off some of their original requirements for a new feature to which they are suddenly introduced—a stone fireplace, or panelled dining-room, or swimming pool. Perhaps a sudden fad has sprung up for patios, for double glass sliding doors, or, going further back, for recreation rooms, split levels, built-in bars, wall-to-wall broadloom or "California" breakfast nooks.

The third factor which determines the destination of move is information. A searching household may be aware of only a fraction of the housing available: the houses nearby, or on the way to work, or where their friends live. The limitations of time and the deadline for moving restrict the time for looking and further reduce the number of available opportunities. This rather haphazard search procedure is even more true of moves which do not involve house purchase: the shifts among boarding houses or apartments or any rental accommodation are often by word-of-mouth or window signs.

Each of the three factors—demand, supply and the search process—help define neighbourhood characteristics. Ability to pay and the kind of housing required by the consumer interact with developer decisions to determine income and life cycle variations. The information and interaction patterns tend to strengthen ethnic and life style clusters. Through these rather imperfect processes the spatial pattern of the various social groups emerges. Highly specialized areas such as skid row or the most exclusive street in town came about because the people inhabiting these areas have very specific needs, and because the alternative choices are very closely grouped in space.

The social differences among urban neighbourhoods continue and show no sign of decline. If anything, differences are becoming more clearly delineated as the number of live-in servants is declining, and housing is less and less shared by different generations. We live in the age of highly specialized housing—the retirement bungalows for elderly persons on $250 to $300 pensions, the cottage designed precisely for 2 parents, 3 children and a cat.

The urban dweller prefers it that way. On his narrow lot or in the corridor of his apartment he is at the mercy of his neighbours. If they do not share his feelings about the appropriateness or inappropriateness of holding late parties, sunbathing on the lawn, or parking hot rods in front of the house, they worry him to death. There is no way to escape constant contact with, or at least awareness of, people nearby. This is

147

forcibly brought home to the essentially private person who has lived downtown with his own circle of friends, and then moves into a house in an area where block parties and over-the-fence exchanges with neighbours are the accepted mode.

So the developer who lays out various subdivisions, and the city planner who drafts the zoning by-laws, combine to keep each group apart. Rich and poor, young and old are carefully segregated by blocks of non-residential land use or even parks if necessary.

Keeping ethnic groups apart is more difficult. Laws prevent overt discrimination and ethnicity cuts across age and income levels. But realtors still tend to steer different people into different areas, and it becomes rapidly known that such and such a subdivision is Jewish, while another one is aimed at the Italian market. "Oh, I don't think you'd really like that area", is the secret but universally understood password to social homogeneity. Young executives or salesmen with families who move often can rely on the realtor to relocate them in a neighbourhood in the new city exactly like the one they left.

BOISSEVAIN, Jeremy, *The Italians of Montreal: Social Adjustment in a Plural Society,* Study No. 7 of the Royal Commission on Bilingualism and Biculturalism (Ottawa: Queen's Printer, 1970).

CLARK, S. D., *The Suburban Society* (Toronto: University of Toronto Press, 1966). How the suburbs develop.

GANS, Herbert, *The Levittowners* (New York: Pantheon Books, 1967). A participant observer in a large U.S. suburban development.

GOLANT, Stephen, *The Residential Location and Spatial Behavior of the Elderly* (Chicago: University of Chicago, Department of Geography, Research Paper No. 143, 1972).

HUGHES, Everett C., *French Canada in Transition* (Chicago: University of Chicago Press, 1941). A study of the social structure of Drummondville, Quebec in the thirties.

KATZ, Michael, "The People of a Canadian City, 1851-2," *Canadian Historical Review,* LIII (December, 1972), pp. 402-426. The social structure of Hamilton, Ontario, a century ago.

KELLER, Suzanne, *The Urban Neighbourhood* (New York: Random House, 1968). What we know and don't know about the neighbourhood and its role in urban life.

LIEBERSON, S., "Bilingualism in Montreal: A Demographic Analysis," *American Journal of Sociology,* LXXI (July, 1965), pp. 10-25. Describes the degree of French and English speaking segregation.

MICHELSON, William H., *Man and His Urban Environment* (Toronto: Addison-Wesley, 1970). A Toronto-based sociologist looks at how different kinds of people behave in various urban environments.

MURDIE, Robert A., *Factorial Ecology of Metropolitan Toronto, 1951-1961* (Chicago: University of Chicago, Department of Geography, Research Paper No. 116, 1969). The classic study of sectors, rings and nodes.

PORTER, John, *The Vertical Mosaic* (Toronto: University of Toronto Press, 1965). The major variants of Canadian society and who gets where.

SEELEY, John R., SIM, R. Alexander, and LOOSELEY, E. W., *Crestwood Heights: A Study of the Culture of Suburban Life* (Toronto: University of Toronto Press, 1956). Actually, a study of life in Forest Hill, an upper-income neighbourhood in Toronto.

WEIR, Thomas R., "A Survey of the Day-time Population of Winnipeg," *Queen's Quarterly* LXVII (Winter, 1961), pp. 654-62. The distribution of workers, students and shoppers during the day.

ZORBAUGH, H. W., *The Gold Coast and the Slum* (Chicago: University of Chicago Press, 1929).

149

8 The Changing City

Throughout this book we've talked of change. Change is the heart of urban Canada. Not only are cities the principal agents and locations of change for the country, but the city itself is always in motion: growing, adjusting, decaying, re-developing. An endless flow of people in and out and within the city generates continuous social change, while the births and deaths of business enterprises, the continual investments in new facilities and modifications of the old, transform the physical landscape.

As each city blooms and evolves, different components change at different rates. The turnover of people may be very high in an area catering to transients, yet the basic social patterns of that area remain remarkably stable. Buildings stay in use for a rapid succession of enterprises. A trail blazed at the beginning of permanent settlement may be unaltered in course (still with that irritating bend before the bridge) but transformed now from a forest path to a neon-blazing commercial ribbon.

At any one point in time the city we examine is only a very quick snapshot of a city in motion—a snapshot which is useful not for its description of the city now, as it becomes outdated so rapidly, but for its insight into what the city was and what it is becoming. The old areas, the empty areas, and the developing areas are indicators of a pattern of change.

During the development of each city, decisions made in different times for different reasons created the context for

8.1 Sources of Change

The evolution of urban Canada results from the cumulation of new technology, new institutions, and the increased prosperity of Canadians. Here are some of the milestones. The growths in income levels and automobile ownership accelerate the impact of some of these innovations, as well as creating effects of their own.

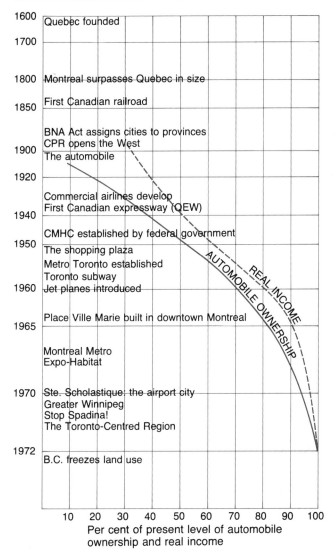

1600	Quebec founded
1700	
1800	Montreal surpasses Quebec in size
1850	First Canadian railroad
1900	BNA Act assigns cities to provinces CPR opens the West
	The automobile
1920	
1940	Commercial airlines develop First Canadian expressway (QEW)
1950	CMHC established by federal government
	The shopping plaza Metro Toronto established Toronto subway
1960	Jet planes introduced
1965	Place Ville Marie built in downtown Montreal
	Montreal Metro Expo-Habitat
1970	Ste. Scholastique: the airport city Greater Winnipeg Stop Spadina! The Toronto-Centred Region
1972	
	B.C. freezes land use

AUTOMOBILE OWNERSHIP

REAL INCOME

10 20 30 40 50 60 70 80 90 100

Per cent of present level of automobile ownership and real income present-day changes. In the same way the expressways, the subdivisions and parks presently under construction will be used for decades and shape other investments still to come. Just as 19th-century Montreal can be recreated from the buildings and streets that remain today, the Montreal of the 21st century can be anticipated by examining the existing structure and projecting new elements to come with future urban forces.

Predicting the future of a Canadian city is not an exercise in science fiction. Perhaps fifty per cent of urban Canada in the year 2000 already exists. Factories, office buildings, expressways, and especially property lines and land uses, usually survive for fifty to a hundred years. Another large part of our future cities will be built within the next ten or fifteen years under conditions much like today—the same institutions of land tenure and financing, the same circulation pattern, the same kinds of personal preferences.

As we get further and further into the future, though, the basic forces determining city form and city life will become more and more different and unpredictable. Demography, income, personal mobility, technology, and personal preferences all have a variety of effects on the way of life and physical problems of the city. But many of the changes will be changes of proportion rather than innovation. More office workers, fewer factory workers; more shopping plazas, fewer corner stores.

Let us first evaluate some changes in the variables affecting urban form, and then discuss the possible outcomes, that is, take a look at the city of the future. One of the most significant factors altering the cityscape is the increased income of the inhabitants, although its effect is often lumped in with the general processes of urban growth. (Growth will continue to modify the city, but since the effects of size can be observed right now, in various stages, we shall not consider it in detail). Another area of change is technology, including both the radical innovations like the jet belt or the moving sidewalks, which get all the attention, and the regular incremental improvements in expressway systems, sewage plants and building construction. Potentially the most powerful agents of change are our social and political institutions—changes in tax structure, units of government and attitudes towards the family.

Rising Incomes

Over the last fifty years, perhaps longer, the average yearly increase in real income in Canadian cities has been one to two per cent. Every twenty or thirty years the standard of living doubles for most urban Canadians. This increased income is derived from many sources: growth of the internal economy, technical changes, higher education, more capital; but for whatever reason, the effects are enormous.

Consider housing. Higher incomes for all social classes permit Canadians to purchase better housing—newer, more spacious and of better quality. Housing abandoned by upper class groups filters down to middle-class families, who can also pay more. Affluence enables people to move out of their rental accommodation or row housing and buy four-bedroom ranch houses in the suburbs. Higher wages mean the latest and "best" apartments are always filled. The very worst housing is abandoned. It becomes so unattractive that it is economically less productive than rebuilding.

If one uses a fixed standard of housing condition, unchanging over time, the proportion of poor housing in Canada decreased in the last two decades despite the rapid rate of growth which increased demand for all types of housing. Most of the improvement is due to private redevelopment, since very few Canadian urban renewal projects have been undertaken. The continuing rise in living standards means a rise in the standard of minimum housing. Conditions accepted as normal a generation ago are now a cause for public alarm.

The same rise in standards affects other types of land use. Consumers expect better stores; workers want better factories and offices. If you've eaten in ancient restaurants in stagnant small towns you know the feeling; the relative obsolescence of many elements in the rural landscape is one of the reasons for going to the city. Higher wages shift consumer expenditure from one activity to another. High labour-consuming activities—shoe repairs, hat blocking and so on—are replaced by outlets selling new goods. Secondhand stores give way to boutiques.

The public also expects higher standards (and higher expenditures) in education and recreation as their incomes increase. Superhighways, airports, and universities satisfy needs which the average person could not afford even 40 years ago. People with higher incomes become particular about zoning, about traffic and utilities. More students stay in school; more parents expect better education and better trained teachers; teachers, too, want a higher standard of living. The result is a spiral in public expenditure, and a new kind of city.

Urban growth has accompanied income changes for the last twenty years. Growth has meant that the thrust for improving quality has been partially diverted to coping with the need for increases in quantity, particularly in the public sector. Municipalities are trying to provide more school space and to acquire sufficient teachers, and so have less time or funds to rethink and improve the educational programme. At the same time, however, growth provides the justification and capital for tearing down and rebuilding, for building new facilities in tune with today's needs, for promoting younger, more innovative people to positions of responsibility, and for changing urban boundaries and urban government.

New Technology

Income increases and growth work hand in hand with technological change by making automation more desirable economically, increasing the rate of obsolescence, and providing the funds for the purchase of cars and downtown parking.

Technological change has led to certain kinds of urban change and accelerated others, but always in conjunction with economic changes. Investment capital and the promise of a future prosperity are required to create a railway, no matter how many people stand ready to sell you trains. The steel frame, concrete shell building and the elevator made mass apartment living possible, but a high level of consumer demand was required to produce the present-day profusion of high-rise apartments.

One of the outstanding examples of the impact of mass technology is the automobile. But it was not so much the internal combustion engine as the mass production procedures and the rise of personal income which permitted every family to own a car; and, in turn, transformed the urban landscape. The automobile lies behind virtually every recent change in the physical form of the city. It is a personal transportation system, not tied to the public transport network, and by eliminating the time spent in walking, waiting, and transferring, the access pattern of the city has been drastically modified.

Even the most heavily travelled area of the city, the central business district, is much closer to everyone in terms of travel time. Twenty-eighth street is as close in terms of time as fourteenth street used to be, and twenty-eighth street has much more space at lower rents. The city can decentralize—move out farther in distance—but stay close in time. Rents decline in the most central areas. Gradually a new process sets in; it becomes less important to be near the centre at all. A public transit system gives good service only towards downtown; a trip on the periphery is well-nigh impossible. But for a man with a car it is much easier to drive around the rim than go towards the centre. Why not work, shop, and play in outlying parts of the city, areas farther apart but easier to reach than the old city centre?

And so, over time, the attraction of the urban core has declined. Suburban dwellers travel in all directions for the services they need. Many hardly ever go downtown. The new urban structure is of lower density, with more open spaces, more vacant areas. An extra half-mile is hell for a pedestrian, painful to a bus-rider, but only a few seconds further for a motorist on a suburban arterial or freeway.

The grouping of activities, the scale of design of buildings and sites, has jumped a whole order of magnitude to the pace of the automobile. No one walks into or around a big shopping plaza. The entrance to the plaza and access to the buildings are designed for the automobile. New suburban areas already present a 21st-century appearance. All services, all routes, all buildings, are designed for riders, not walkers. The whole environment—signals, scenery, vantage points—is for people travelling at 30 to 40 miles an hour. Contrast it with the density and diversity of entrances, signs and symbols, or the size of alleys or building lots, in the old city centre.

Ultimately, of course, the old parts of the city are forced to compromise. Large areas are levelled for parking lots. Overhead freeways or wide arterial streets separate smaller pedestrian-size clusters of activities. Gradually downtown is no longer the only node of the city, but just one of many; a specialized district where activities requiring face-to-face contact, and certain kinds of services, are provided: the financial area, the cheapest or most expensive stores. A greater and greater part of the ordinary urban action occurs elsewhere.

With the takeover of the automobile has also come, paradoxically, a new awareness of the needs of pedestrians. Suburban and downtown shopping plazas are now constructing enclosed malls, or interior pedestrian walkways where children are safe from traffic, even provided with playgrounds, while mothers shop in a cool (or heated) and relaxed environment.

A much greater separation of pedestrian and vehicular activities seems indicated for urban centres—perhaps underground or elevated streets, complete separation of parking and travelling facilities, and multilevel pedestrian walkways in high-density core areas.

The recognition of pedestrian needs may turn change, as so often happens, back on itself, resulting in a modification of the car that began it all. If the division of pedestrian-vehicular activities proves too uneconomical a solution to the problem of noise, space, fumes, and dirt, the car itself will have to be made cleaner, quieter, and smaller. The small electric-powered, golf-cart car designed specifically and exclusively for high-density central core areas may become a viable economic alternative; the small car might be made for storing in or towing behind conventional cars which would then be left at the parking ring surrounding the central core.

One can muse on a wide variety of possible technological innovations. A favourite Canadian dream is the enclosed dome, to moderate the winters. If the city of the future acquires its own enclosed, air-conditioned atmosphere, considerations of the relative economic feasibility of eliminating carbon monoxide or ozone may determine the fate of the car as we know it.

Other technological changes contribute in lesser ways: improved and cheaper public utilities, better mass transit, new forms of construction, new concepts in recreation, public health or welfare; but none have so far radically altered the urban life style. And it is difficult to anticipate areas of significant technological innovation in the future. Moving sidewalks, plastic prefab homes, automated retailing, or independent utility systems for each dwelling are some of the more probable suggestions.

Institutional Change

However, the major changes will probably result not from physical, but from institutional improvements. The increasing size of corporations leads to a larger and more economical scale of development as products are standardized. Improved internal communications permit the decentralization of different components of large firms: manufacturing in one part of the city, executive offices downtown, and salesmen widely scattered. Already there are signs of other forms of institutional change of great significance, such as the alteration of urban government.

For 50 to 100 years, the city has been governed by provincial laws which were developed for small towns and rural townships. The boundaries and size of the city were assumed to be relatively constant and its duties limited to the provision of a standard and minimal set of services. But cities are growing rapidly, and expanding in space even more rapidly, consuming nearby townships and villages at alarming speeds. The metropolis is an intensely interacting unity, yet each of these small municipalities, governed in this traditional form, often by the same traditional rurally oriented people, has sovereignty over an arbitrary part of the city. As a result, a hodge-podge of different jurisdictions, different laws, and different levels of services emerges. Perhaps the most serious difficulty is the widely differing economic bases for municipal services. How do you educate children to the standard high school level when one suburb has 100 million dollars in factories and only 1,000 homes, while another is using the limited tax base provided by 10,000 working-class dwellings? How does a rural municipality suddenly generate the capital required to service 20,000 new homes?

Further stresses are provided by the increased expectations from municipal governments, expressed mainly through the pressures exerted on them by other levels of government. Originally the duty of the municipality was to provide law, order and justice. This slowly expanded to include education and public utilities, and now demands are made for a wide range of health and welfare activities as well as for more direct control over environmental and cultural conditions. Civic fathers are increasingly held responsible for the whole urban image—growth and progress, square or swinging.

The growing responsibilities and the expanding size of urban areas call for a new kind of municipal government. Already some new forms are being tried. Ontario leans toward massive annexation in which a city absorbs whole townships at a time. New Brunswick has gone furthest, adopting a scheme whereby the province takes over all financial responsibilities of local municipalities. A regional government dispenses funds.

In Ontario and in Winnipeg, a second level of municipal government has been established, the metropolitan government. Metro Toronto, set up by Ontario in 1953, took over many duties of the local municipalities requiring high capital expenditures, such as physical services. The city and suburban municipalities continue to operate within the larger metropolitan structure. The Ontario government has followed up with several other regional governments.

Metro Toronto was sufficiently successful to justify the allocations of greater responsibilities to the Metropolitan government in 1966 while amalgamating the member municipalities into 6 boroughs. In some areas, particularly the provision of roads, utilities and educational facilities required for metropolitan growth, and in their continuing financial support, Metro has been the most successful experiment of its kind in North America.

The experience in social programmes such as welfare and in the more aesthetic amenities of urban life has been less successful, wrecked by internal jealousies and conflicts which lead ultimately to no action. Also, as Metro's responsibilities

159

increase there is more and more dissatisfaction with some features of its structure, particularly the indirect representation which makes it difficult for the citizen to affect Metro policies directly. Metro council members are designated from borough Councils and they themselves elect a full-time chairman. The voter gets to choose only his borough member.

Metropolitan institutions show the possibilities for institutional innovation, the range of choices available to a community, the alternative levels of spatial and functional integration which can be chosen. Government can serve a neighbourhood or suburb, or a whole region; it can deal with subways and highways and schools at once, or it can solve each problem in isolation.

Other trends of change concern less formal institutions. More women work, which expands the labour force; there are fewer children, which affects housing needs and leisure activities; more old people have better pensions and social services, which creates a demand for specialized housing in special locations. Better communications systems and scientific management may lead to larger corporations; anti-authoritarian attitudes by workers demand smaller, decentralized work groups; more functions of the private sector may be transferred to the public sector, such as transportation of all kinds, leisure activities, and housing. Indirectly, these trends change the shape of a city, altering the mix of housing, or the location of offices, or the inter-urban patterns of growth.

Each level of economic or cultural organization—continental, national, regional—inspires a new pattern of variation in cities. Should the citizens of Halifax drink Schlitz or Molson's or Moosehead beer? The Canadian Radio-Television Commission can also shape life-styles in urban Canada by deciding whether Brandon watches "Hee Haw," or "Stompin' Tom Connors," or the Manitoba Wranglers.

160

The Predictions

Figure 8.2 predicts the population growth paths of major Canadian cities, based on the current economic and demographic patterns and the recent history of growth. In the foreseeable future practically all the growth in Canada is going to be concentrated in a few dozen very small (in area) locations. Here we have one of the most significant aspects of urban Canada, and the prime reason for trying to understand it. Much capital investment, many innovations, and a great deal of conflict will accompany this growth. The stress of spatial adjustment to a changing world will take place in existing urban communities—in the Annex in Toronto, in the Glebe in Ottawa, in the East End in Vancouver.

The cities of Calgary, Edmonton, Vancouver, and Victoria will continue to absorb the drift of population from the East to the West. Toronto, Montreal, and Vancouver will bear the brunt of movement from smaller centres to larger metropolitan areas. Ottawa has always absorbed the continuing shift in employment from the forest and factory to the committee room and the typing pool. Sudbury, dependent on the international nickel market, is largely unpredictable (but we've tried).

If Regina, Saskatoon, and Winnipeg grow as indicated, but within provinces that will grow very little, the implication is a massive transfer of people and facilities from the small towns and villages all over the West to these few centres.

Saint John and St. John's are unlikely to grow very much at all, probably less than 50,000 persons apiece. Their present economy, the areas they serve, and the amenities they offer are not part of the wave of the future. Neither workers, nor industrialists, nor tourists are interested.

The degree of change within each city is suggested by

161

8.2 Population: Past Growth and Future Forecasts

The actual population statistics for census metropolitan areas are given for 1961 and 1971. All data refer to the census metropolitan areas as defined in 1966. Data obtained from N. Harvey Lithwick, *Urban Canada: Problems and Prospects,* Report to the Minister of State for Urban Affairs, No. 5 (Ottawa: Information Canada, 1970), p. 108.

(000's)	1961	1971	1981	1991	2001
Calgary	279	403	437	544	705
Edmonton	339	487	536	675	881
Halifax	184	205	255	324	421
Hamilton	395	489	626	798	1031
Kitchener	155	227	293	384	504
London	181	236	279	349	452
Montreal	2111	2587	3568	4738	6346
Ottawa	430	555	680	870	1138
Quebec	358	463	562	700	891
Regina	112	140	169	210	275
St. John's	92	112	113	124	136
Saint John	96	102	123	148	184
Saskatoon	96	126	159	198	250
Sudbury	111	145	144	178	223
Toronto	1825	2465	3309	4487	6128
Vancouver	790	1027	1224	1560	2026
Victoria	154	196	244	304	389
Windsor	193	238	280	346	432
Winnipeg	477	540	620	751	932

the increase in population. In thirty years Toronto will look like Chicago today, Vancouver will look like Toronto, and London and Halifax will look like Ottawa. Saint John's appearance will change very slowly, only as old buildings are replaced, or when its citizens gradually upgrade their housing as levels of income increase. It will take some major outside force to alter the present basic pattern. In Vancouver, by contrast, the areas of land used in housing, in stores, and in industry, will more than double in the next thirty years. Urban activities will compete for more space, offices will encroach on residential neighbourhoods, and new roads and sewers will uproot established parks and boulevards. This table delineates the major frontiers—or frontlines—of tomorrow.

BOURNE, Larry S., MacKINNON, R. D., SIEGEL, J., and SIM-MONS, J. W. (eds.), *Urban Futures for Central Canada* (Toronto: University of Toronto Press, 1974). Forecasts and implications for the future for the cities of Ontario and Quebec.

DIAMOND, A. J., "The New City," *Habitat* X, 1 (January-February, 1967), pp. 33-40. Experimental urban designs.

DRAPER, James A. (ed.), *Citizen Participation: Canada* (Toronto: New Press, 1971).

KAPLAN, Harold, *The Regional City* (Toronto: Canadian Broadcasting Corporation, 1965). Existing forms of local government and the pressures upon them.

POWELL, Alan (ed.), *The City: Attacking the Modern Myths* (Toronto: McClelland and Stewart, 1972). A series of articles, Toronto-based, presenting different views of what urban life should be.

RACINE, Jean-Bernard, "Exurbanisation et métamorphisme péri-urbain," *Révue de Géographie de Montréal,* XXI, 2 (1967), pp. 313-342. A case study of the effect of Montreal on a small village in the Eastern Townships.

RICHARDSON, Boyce, *The Future of Canadian Cities* (Toronto: New Press, 1972). A countrywide review of current issues facing urban Canada.

SMALLWOOD, Frank, *Metro Toronto: A Decade Later* (Toronto: Bureau of Municipal Research, 1963). A review of the accomplishments of an institutional innovation.

YEATES, Maurice, *The Windsor to Quebec City Axis* (Montreal: McGill-Queen's University Press, 1974). Descriptions and forecasts of Canada's main urban concentration.

9 Issues and Policy Making

Our urban environment is an important part of our lives. It reflects our culture, yet alters it at the same time. The form of urban Canada is continually changing, with the addition of new jobs, entertainments, architectures, government procedures, and so on. As awareness of the urban environment becomes widespread, Canadians begin to ask, "Can we control the shape of the city and the way people live in it?" and if we can, and if we want to, "What kind of urban life do we want?" Answering these questions is itself a process, a process which reflects the very complex life of a city. As the procedures for consciously shaping the city are developed, such as zoning, urban renewal, and land banks, the problems keep changing. First, it was bad housing downtown, then urban sprawl in the suburbs. Now it is high-rise apartments and impossible housing costs everywhere. Each solution brings new problems.

As the possibilities of integrated urban design broaden to include different densities, land-use mixtures, and ratios of parking lots to parks, making a choice becomes more difficult. The priorities of your grandmother in Welland are not the same as those of the mayor of Kamloops. In fact, they are often opposite. The city's future is determined by first identifying points of agreement among city-dwellers, then by making complex trade-offs between the alternatives: a little better bus service, a few more street widenings.

The result of such compromises is a highly standardized future path for Canadian cities from Prince Rupert to

St. John's: growth, but at a controlled rate; higher personal income, but not much redistribution from rich to poor; a prosperous downtown and automobile-oriented suburbs. Either by choice or necessity, the planning goals and programmes of most cities are almost identical.

No single decision determines the future urban environment. On the one hand, growth rates of cities reflect the national or international economy. On the other hand, the particular form Prince Albert will take in the years to come depends not only on its growth, but also on the opinions of municipal council members, city engineers, and downtown businessmen, as they deal with issue after issue. And every city-dweller helps shape his own neighbourhood, by gracing it with his presence, by selling out to someone richer or poorer or of a different ethnic origin, by building a new porch, or by signing a petition against street parking.

Urban Canada in the year 2000 will be the product of many, many decisions by all sorts of people and institutions. Most of the decisions are not consciously directed to the actual effects they will have on the city. They include all the little consumer choices: to drive or walk, to build a house or rent, to spend a weekend in Quebec City or the Laurentians. The indirect actions of governments and organizations are also important: to increase oil exports, to rationalize freight rates, to change the cost of borrowing money.

Urban Life-styles

The diversity of decisions and the fact that all of us are ultimately involved in making them restrict the variety of the result. Our urban environments are very simply the expression of our mass culture. "We shape our buildings and they shape us." A radical change in our cities requires a social revolution affecting in a basic way how we earn our bread, define our families, or choose our leisure patterns. This basic cultural dependency, along with the considerable existing investment in buildings, roads, and utilities, guarantees a gradual evolution of the urban landscape. More, yes, but more of the same.

Cities and cultures evolve gradually, as one generation replaces another: attitudes to drinking change slowly, the population becomes better educated, a younger mayor takes office, the old police chief retires, a new high school is built with a theatre and a swimming pool. As each replacement is selected a city is reshaped. Cities change with respect to each other only as the change in generations is accelerated by rapid growth or a major turnover in the kind of people who live in them.

Because the process of change is similar, different cities tend to make the same choices at the same time. The same kinds of people—young, old, rich, poor—live in each city, and they all get up in the morning and brush their teeth, and watch the national news at night. It is unlikely that in any one city any large number of them will suddenly start living in communes, growing their own gardens, or preferring opera to hockey.

Because Canadians are a mobile lot, the mixture of lifestyles found in each city tends to be very much the same: a number of sports fans, some chess players, several hundred devout beer-drinkers, and a few restless souls who move from yoga to macramé to organic foods. When people of such fundamentally similar habits are served by corporations which are national, or even international, in scope, a further uniformity is imposed. Eaton's, Simpsons, Hudson's Bay, Esso, Gulf, and A & W all play a large part in our urban scene. And

166

increasingly, the development corporations, such as Fairview, Markborough, and Campeau, are operating on a national level, too, imposing the same kinds of apartment houses and shopping malls on North Battleford and North Bay. The same designs, the same materials, and the same economic conditions exist all across the land. You can build a redwood deck in the Maritimes, or a mock Tudor mansion on the prairies.

Although statistically our group decisions are predictable, we are all individuals, and the process of creating the similar nation-city is complex, particular, and stress-filled. When many people live close together within a small area, day-to-day conflicts are inevitable. The bickering is accentuated when people are related in so many ways. People are affected directly or psychologically by the actions of the residents of their buildings, the salaries of the garbage men, the traffic on a main street, or the costs of schools. Any change in the scheme of things inevitably transfers benefits from one group to another: more parks for you, more taxes for me; your dog can play in the park, my kids get dung on their shoes. It is a tribute to the tolerance of urban-dwellers and to their ability to separate individuals from the interests of the various roles they play, that urban living goes on as well as it does. Doctors and patients, Portuguese and West Indians, Cadillac owners and bicyclists can co-exist, even if their interests do not coincide.

It is the fundamental similarities in the behaviour of urban man that create the basis for agreement. We all need water, newspapers, and milk stores. Individual desires tend to be cancelled by the process of choosing. For example, the hankering for an enormous garden is suppressed by the reality of land prices, and hostility towards tax increases is overcome by the odours of a garbage strike.

What we can look for in the future is the increasing impact of urban life on our culture. As more and more of us spend our lives in a high-density, asphalt-coated world, the

167

things we do and the way we do them will continue to be modified by this environment. We will become spectators instead of participants. Fifteen thousand people can watch hockey in the Forum. To let them all play would require converting most of Montreal into ice rinks. City-dwellers choose activities that involve people but don't use space; chess instead of gardening, reading rather than tuba playing, or talking instead of horseback riding.

The urban life-style allows individual variety, but only up to a point. The majority rules in matters affecting large numbers of people. One soon learns to adapt and enjoy less expensive gestures. And the restriction of space is more than offset by the very great increase in possibilities. People move to cities because there is more to do there. The urban environment modifies their physical behaviour, but it enlarges their spirit.

The Decision-making Process

When large numbers of people with very different desires try to create a common environment to live in, certain points of disagreement are bound to occur. Other conflicts arise because basically similar people live in different locations. Region is pitted against region, city against city, community against community. These conflicts are part of the process of determining the future city. When the Opposition squawks in Parliament, or the Premiers thunder at Dominion-Provincial conferences, or irate ratepayers march on city council, the choice mechanism is operating.

What is happening now is a shift from implicit decisions

in the market to conscious debates in the public sector. It used to be that when they closed the factory in your town, you had the choice of moving or starving. Or if they bought your neighbour's house to build a parking garage, you could sell, too, or lump it. Now you can stand and fight. Whether you win or lose, a lot of interesting points of view will be evident in the process.

The nature and location of power increasingly fascinates people. Who makes the decisions about various aspects of urban life? Who should participate in the decision making? The fundamental decisions about what city grows or does not grow can really only be made at a national level. The main trends of population redistribution are occurring among provinces. Halifax cannot grow if Nova Scotia does not. Victoria must grow even if the province of British Columbia and the local council are unenthusiastic. This inability to influence such a basic aspect of urban life creates a great deal of dissatisfaction at junior levels of government. The same restrictions, however, occur in other situations. The province, by means of its legislation on zoning and other planning controls and its support for urban services, governs the basic form of its cities. Calgary, Kitchener, and Shawinigan have no power to overrule these restrictions. Decisions about annexations, new sewers, and schools are made outside the power of local citizens. Neighbourhoods in turn must appeal to city councils or provincial departments for support in their efforts to change traffic patterns or restrict land uses.

As urban Canada grows, the power of urban-based politicians grows and changes. Anti-Montreal legislation faces the wrath of twenty-five Members of Parliament and three Cabinet Ministers. The shift to metropolitan government reduces the variation in the urban form of Ottawa, e.g., a homogeneous policy representing the joint interests of Rockcliffe and Vanier City replaces the eccentricities of ten different local councils. In general, as the policy at any one level

169

becomes closely coordinated, the power of the individual unit—either city or neighbourhood—to determine its environment independently, declines.

The result need not be homogeneity. The integration of financial resources across a metropolitan area can allow some sections of the city to grow and others to stay the same, relieved of the necessity of hustling after new property tax sources. An area-wide school system can afford some very specialized educational services. The City of Winnipeg exhibits far more variation from neighbourhood to neighbourhood than all the autonomous prairie towns put together.

Each of the three main levels of urban environment— the nation-city, the individual city, and the neighbourhood— has its own particular scope for change, its own issues, powers, and interest groups. In the following three sections, we'll look at the issues unique to each level.

In addition to the conflicts among levels of the urban environment, there are conflicts among different groups or sectors within these levels, such as the rich and the poor, the young and the old, the downtown and the suburbs. For example, although the city as a whole may pursue the goal of moderate growth, different neighbourhoods will fight the new airport or the sewage plant, which growth requires.

Issues of the Nation-City

It is within the realm of policy to determine how various benefits or disbenefits of our society should be distributed among the cities of Canada. Policy answers the following questions: Which cities should grow and which should not?

What services or facilities should be provided to all urban residents? Should income levels of the residents of St. John's differ from those of St. Jérôme any more or less than the wages of a carpenter differ from those of a mechanic? Should our cities become more alike or more diverse?

Regional income differences, problems of growth here and decline there, and the helplessness of small cities and regions whose future seems to be controlled by outside forces, are traditional concerns in Canada. Royal Commissions and academics have long studied these subjects, but only recently has federal and provincial public policy been applied to the problems. Besides making use of the traditional tools of industrial location incentives and public works programmes, it is possible to channel the whole weight of the federal budget —over 15 billion dollars per year—to solving these problems. It is also possible to control tariffs and the export of resources, to control immigration, and to develop policies for pensions or welfare payments, all with the single view of shaping a new urban landscape in Canada.

Nevertheless, governments are not omnipotent. Practical bounds exist on what can be done. They can decide which of the prairie cities should grow, but they cannot alter the fundamental economy of the region. Although all new public investment could be focussed at one or two locations ("growth points" in the current jargon), vigorous protests would arise from competing cities.

The decision to interfere in the urban landscape can be politically very painful. Competition between cities is very great; London will not rejoice at Sarnia's improvement. Governments must be convinced that reducing inequities among cities rates a higher priority than eliminating problems of bad housing or social class differences within cities. Can the problems of life in declining cities like Rouyn, Quebec, or Summerside, P.E.I., be justified by the increased overall standard of living of Canadians? Are the two related?

Figure 9.1 illustrates the very rough relationship between growth rate and level of income. With the notable exception of Chicoutimi, the more prosperous places are also the rapidly growing ones. With some reason, cities believe that without growth they are not getting a fair share of the nation's wealth. Presumably government policy is aimed at reducing the variations in the diagram and approximating equal growth rates and wage levels throughout the country.

In anticipation of increased interest in urban policy at the national level during the seventies, let us suggest a few other principles. First, efforts should be made to let people live where they want. Jobs should be created in these areas, rather than in some tundra community where copper ore happens to be and where life can be made barely tolerable.

Second, instead of attacking bigness or smallness, efforts should be made to regulate rates of growth. It is the very high rate of growth that leads to inflated housing costs, servicing problems, and the disruption of old neighbourhoods. It is the decline in the rate of growth that leads to the painful out-migration of older settled people because of their inability to get work.

Third, all citizens should be given equal access to certain kinds of public facilities and services, such as universities, specialized medical care, subsidized cultural events, and the like. If the university is located in Halifax, then students from Sydney should get free room and board. Patients from Brandon should be transported free to the clinics in Winnipeg. The residents of Pembroke should not have to pay transportation costs to enjoy events at the National Arts Centre in Ottawa.

Finally, in order to broaden the choice available, there seems to be some merit in maintaining as great a diversity as possible in cities in terms of size, the physical environment, and life-style. A well-developed range of city sizes in each major region of Canada would be a good objective.

172

9.1 Inequities in the Nation City

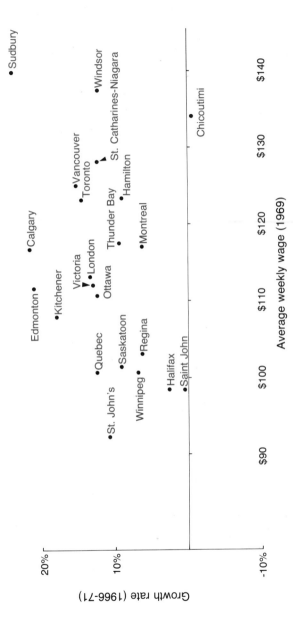

Data obtained from Statistics Canada, *Employment Earnings and Hours*, July-September, 1971.

Unfortunately, these policies frequently contradict each other. In Parliament, where members represent spatial constituencies, it is difficult to favour one region consistently over another. But most of all, it is difficult to gain the attention of national policy makers. Other issues—defense, inflation, unemployment, national unity—tend to have priority over the pursuit of policies aimed solely at a better distribution of urban centres. The forecasts of the previous chapter may be accelerated or delayed in time, but the relative sizes of cities have little chance of change through policy.

The Future of City X

Whatever the good intentions of the federal or provincial governments, a particular policy may not be the best solution for City X. Its citizens may wish it to grow more rapidly in order to provide certain municipal services for its residents. A more diversified local economy may be required to provide jobs for all its offspring. The city may be run by the kind of boosters who prefer attractions for tourists to services for its citizens. What kinds of options exist for City X?

A paramount concern of many Canadian cities is economic growth. Growth helps pay off the debentures for municipal facilities, it ensures jobs for the unemployed, it makes the local merchants prosperous, and generally creates an atmosphere in which ambitious young people thrive. At the same time, growth leads to a demand for new services, it creates more debt, and it uproots neighbourhoods. Unfortunately, control of growth is largely beyond a city's means. It requires outside capital and outside markets, and the city must be more efficient than other centres. A policy of no growth means that life in Hamilton must be made so intolerable, in terms of unemployment, housing costs, or traffic jams, that newcomers will not come.

A city has the most control over all the intimate details which affect the daily lives of its citizens—homeowners' feelings of security in their neighbourhoods, their sense of safety in the street, the degree to which noise, or smells, or high taxes infringe on their serenity. The daily environment evolves gradually through many decisions over time, and probably reflects a local cultural consensus, tempered by the international experience in sewer construction, library services, or elementary school teaching techniques. However, a bias towards certain kinds of outcomes could gradually change the atmosphere of a city and distinguish it as a better place to live, at least for certain kinds of people.

Cities can determine their own priorities at this level (see Figure 9.2). Consider the city that "goes for green" by voting for more parks on every budget conflict, by choosing trees over wider roads, by sponsoring flower gardens instead of beauty contests. Another city may have a singleminded concern for cheap housing, administered by means of land banks, public assistance for housing, tolerant zoning, and rigid building code enforcement. Another city might decide for an all-out free enterprise system with an absolute minimum of social controls in the hope of maximizing total income; a further possibility would be to establish a highly selective community in which only high-paying white collar activities were welcome.

Most decisions in City X tend to be conservative, reinforcing the existing pattern. Many expenditures are decided by a rule of thumb, e.g., last year's budget plus 7 per cent. Decisions about servicing an area must be made in the context of the present system, for example, a new school must fit into the existing pattern of schools, or a one-way street must satisfy

175

9.2 **Make a Choice**

An urban environment is the result of hundreds of decisions. A change in the city requires a constant bias in the choice made. The alternatives suggested here are typical.

1. Spend the last $100,000 in the city budget on one of the following:
   a. a new playground in a middle-class area
   b. widening a street corner where two accidents occurred last month
   c. two new garbage trucks
   d. a national campaign to attract new industry
   e. a new roof on city hall
2. Hire a new city employee to fill one of the following posts:
   a. a teacher who will develop a school programme for learning disabilities
   b. a policeman specially trained to work in immigrant areas
   c. a computer expert to reorganize the city purchasing office
   d. a research assistant for the mayor
3. Devote your spare time for the next month to:
   a. stopping an expressway
   b. electing a friend to the school board
   c. protesting a rezoning to higher density
   d. getting a crossing guard for the neighbourhood school
4. Choose a place to live:
   a. a four-bedroom ranch style, six miles from downtown
   b. a two-bedroom high-rise apartment, within walking distance of downtown
   c. an older duplex, two miles from downtown, with lots of trees
   d. a three-bedroom townhouse, ten miles from downtown, plus one month at a nearby lakeside cottage
5. Vote for or against:
   a. a ratepayers' association proposal to revoke a rezoning for a service station

b. a city-funded land bank to eliminate speculation in suburban land
c. a study for a new expressway to encircle downtown
d. a merger of police, social workers, and teachers into a massive department of community affairs
e. the transfer of educational policy making from the school board to neighbourhood committees

6. What should we do with the downtown shopping mall?
It pleases:
a. teenagers
b. tourists
c. parking lot operator A
d. merchants selling records, ice cream, and clothes
It does not please:
a. Baptist ministers
b. the Chief of Police
c. shopping plaza merchants
d. parking lot operator B

the logic of the rest of the circulation pattern. Today's citizens, concerned with their own problems, e.g., taxes and raising children, make decisions which will effect future citizens who will have to live without the hospitals that aren't built, or with the playground that replaces the old fire hall.

When so many interests are involved in making decisions about a city, a critical factor may often be the organizations which allocate power among different groups. What decisions are within the realm of city council or the school board or the YMCA? How are the representatives to each of these bodies elected or appointed? What wards or interest groups do these people represent? Are the wards large or small? How many people vote in the election? Who appoints the university board that spends $10 million a year?

The bias in the institutional structures towards the already favoured citizens of the better residential areas results in programmes and distribution of benefits which are also biased. The first Toronto subway served the high income sector along Yonge Street. Physical improvements to the city are preferred to social services. Other middle-class oriented groups—the Chamber of Commerce, the Association of Women Electors, and the only newspaper in town—supposedly represent the public interest in making decisions.

The average city implements programmes which broadly satisfy the requirements of its more affluent citizens, but it cannot pursue a single goal, like better housing, to the exclusion of other issues. Its citizens are too diverse and have too many needs. The programmes and priorities of cities are growing more and more alike as technical experts and professional managers play a larger role. Standard ratios of parks to people are proclaimed. Minimum qualifications for policemen, social workers, and planners have been set everywhere. For real diversity, we must look within the city.

The Neighbourhood

The power of the individual to shape his city operates only in selective ways. He can choose his environment from the existing diversity, but often his choice will not be among cities but among the various communities within the city. Here is where the variance in life-styles is greatest, and where new ways of living are most likely to be established. Communities continually emerge, which are dominated by people who have similar preferences, and which are quite different from communities a mile or so away. They may be centred around ethnic or religious groups, but, increasingly, they are based on life-styles: the people who live in them are devoted to making money, making wine, or making love.

By far the greatest attention in recent years has been placed on the future of neighbourhoods within the city. Can a neighbourhood formed by change, resist change? If it changes, who decides? What is the role of existing residents? What rights do other residents of the city have? These questions are the outcome of a series of confrontations between neighbourhood groups and larger interests, such as developers, city officials, and other institutions, including the provincial or federal governments. All over the country, people in neighbourhoods of all kinds have organized themselves against plans which appeared to threaten their ways of life. The necessity for expressways and apartment buildings, the best way to expand hospitals or universities, the location and nature of urban renewal schemes, are some of the issues which have been discussed.

Typically, the residents of an area are at first shocked to find that they will have to move, or that the view or noise level or pollution count will be altered. The shock is followed by resentment that the city or an apartment developer could alter an important part of their personal environment without consulting them. The resentment leads to resistance, although sometimes the fight is over before it's begun; the bulldozers move in too fast.

The next stage is a realization of the existence of a real community within the area and a mobilization of its skills to fight off the intruder. This is done through publicity, political influence, and legal means. The community must communicate its point of view as clearly and emphatically as possible. It must denounce the project and the motives of its initiators and link its own interests with the angels. And here, areas where articulate and knowledgeable people reside are at an advantage.

The counterattack will come soon, showing how beneficial the development is to the city as a whole, or at least to several other neighbourhoods. Often an opposition group can be created within the community under attack, made up of people who are quite willing to let the community change and take a profit. Or some "motherhood" principle—"good planning" or "lower taxes"—may be invoked.

As a result of such a confrontation, the community may win, wholly or in compromise, and forestall the apparent fate of the neighbourhood. Once aroused and informed, it can anticipate and respond more quickly to future threats. Once citizens have attended all the planning board and council meetings, and found out how a developer operates, they become aware of all the indicators of change. They can anticipate the alternative uses of their block, sniff out the implications of change of ownership, and follow the sequence of land prices.

Perhaps the most important result is that other communities in the city may become sensitized to community politics. What was a neighbourhood issue—to fight a new apartment development—becomes the broader issue of the preservation of central city neighbourhoods, or, further, a concern for the growth of the entire city. All the city council members relate to the issue to some degree.

The future will see better organized and more articulate representatives of local communities, who can refer to a great body of literature on tactics and theory to back their causes. In some situations, though, the rights and wrongs are complex. Consider the case where neighbourhood A and neighbourhood B both want the single new swimming pool which the town can afford, or where both communities want the city's incinerator located in the other area. Sometimes mutually satisfactory solutions are reached, more often the wealthier, better educated neighbourhood is successful.

In rapidly growing cities, local area residents repeatedly run up against the interests of the city as a whole. Growth requires repeated restructuring of the whole urban fabric—like a snake shedding skins. New arterial roads or sewers or

9.3 Major Postwar Redevelopment in Central Toronto

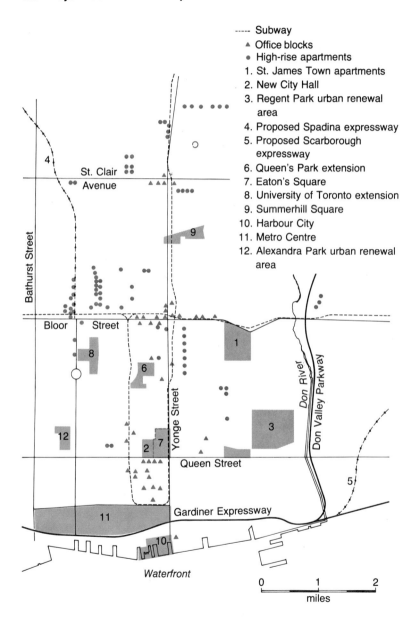

----- Subway
▲ Office blocks
● High-rise apartments
1. St. James Town apartments
2. New City Hall
3. Regent Park urban renewal area
4. Proposed Spadina expressway
5. Proposed Scarborough expressway
6. Queen's Park extension
7. Eaton's Square
8. University of Toronto extension
9. Summerhill Square
10. Harbour City
11. Metro Centre
12. Alexandra Park urban renewal area

hospitals are required, and the rationale for locating them is different for a city of 100,000 than for one of 25,000. The more rapidly the city grows, the more transient the neighbourhoods within it.

Inevitably, neighbourhood attacks neighbourhood. The suburban commuter stalled in traffic curses the downtown resident who protests the new expressway. The deserted wife with three children, whose name is on a public housing waiting list, is not sympathetic to the arguments of suburban matrons. Old establishment areas resist special education programmes for immigrant children.

And if the bulldozers don't raze your community, other processes may. For reasons related to the housing market of the city or the nation, the houses in a neighbourhood may suddenly increase in value so fast, or drop so sharply, that quite different kinds of people move in. Or the expansion of a nearby community may affect another neighbourhood. These kinds of marketplace changes leading to social change in an area are entirely legitimate. In fact, to restrict them would lead to charges of bigotry or segregation. Yet, they are just as effective in changing a community. For example, Don Vale is an old working-class community in Toronto, which has been saved through great effort from high-rise apartment developments on a massive scale (see page 104). Now it is being purchased block by block by professional people who work in downtown Toronto. They evict the roomers, tear down the partitions in the rooms, and are restoring the area to the middle-class preserve that it must have been eighty years ago.

And so it goes. The city grows and changes, but the patterns and processes remain the same. Each generation of residents wants to use the city for its own purposes, but is frustrated by the complexity and peculiar properties of urban life. Cities can be shaped to become more pleasant environments to live in and more suitable to people's needs, but only within the framework of what urban life is really like. Cities cannot recreate rural life or small-town communities. They are a different kind of artifact, and the people who live in them find they must change as the cities change, even as they change the cities.

AXWORTHY, Lloyd and GILLIES, James M. (eds.), *The City: Canada's Prospects, Canada's Problems* (Toronto: Butterworth & Co., 1973). A well-selected series of articles focussing on policy issues.

BUNGE, William, "Urban Nationalism," Discussion Paper B-72-18, Ministry of State for Urban Affairs (Ottawa, 1972). A fascinating discussion of the urbanness of the country, and the need to adjust institutions to this reality. Why should self government in a rural township be the essence of grass roots democracy, while neighbourhood power in a city leads to anarchy?

FIELDMAN, Lionel D. and GOLDRICK, Michael D. (eds.), *Politics and Government of Urban Canada*, 2nd ed. (Toronto: Methuen Publications, 1972). A series of readings which describe governmental institutions and processes operating in urban Canada.

FRASER, Graham, *Fighting Back* (Toronto: A. M. Hakkert, 1972). A blow-by-blow account of the efforts by residents of a poor area in Toronto to affect the urban renewal programme in their neighbourhood.

GRANATSTEIN, J. L., *Marlborough Marathon* (Toronto: A. M. Hakkert, 1971). One street takes on a developer.

METROPOLITAN TORONTO AND REGION TRANSPORTATION STUDY. *Final Report* (Toronto: 1968). Suggests several alternate urban environments—transportation corridors, satellite cities, one big city, and so on.

SEWELL, John, JAFFARY, Karl, KILBOURN, William, and CROMBIE, David, *Inside City Hall* (Toronto: A. M. Hakkert, 1971). This is a series of short articles describing the variety of issues and decisions in the shaping of city T.

Appendix

CANADA'S METROPOLITAN AREAS

	Population (1971)	Site	First Settlement	First Role
Calgary, Alta.	403,000	River	1875	Police post
Chicoutimi, Que.	134,000	River	1676	Fur trade post
Edmonton, Alta.	496,000	River	1795	Settlement node (English)
Halifax, N.S.	223,000	Ocean port	1749	Settlement node
Hamilton, Ont.	499,000	Lake port	1778	Settlement node
Kitchener, Ont.	227,000	River	1800	Settlement node
London, Ont.	286,000	River	1826	Settlement node
Montreal, Que.	2,743,000	River port	1642	Fort and settlement node
St. Catharines-Niagara, Ont.	303,000	River	1796	Fort and portage
Ottawa, Ont.-Que.	602,000	River	1826	Lumbering town
Quebec, Que.	481,000	River port	1608	Fort and settlement node (French)
Regina, Sask.	141,000	Creek	1882	Capital for Northwest Territories
St. John's, Nfld.	132,000	Ocean port	1600	Fishing port
Saint John, N.B.	107,000	River port	1783	Settlement node (Loyalist)
Saskatoon, Sask.	126,000	River	1883	Settlement node
Sudbury, Ont.	155,000	Lake	1883	Minehead
Thunder Bay, Ont.	112,000	Lake	1678	Fur trade post
Toronto, Ont.	2,628,000	Lake port	1750	Fur trade post
Vancouver, B.C.	1,082,000	Ocean port	1827	Fur trade post
Victoria, B.C.	196,000	Ocean port	1843	Fur trade post
Windsor, Ont.	259,000	River port	1750	Settlement node (French)
Winnipeg, Man.	540,000	River	1811	Fur trade post

Male Employment (1961)			Growth (1966-71)	Ethnic Origin (1971)		
Primary and Secondary	*Trade and Service*	*Other*		*English*	*French*	*Other*
22.2%	37.5%	40.3%	21.6%	55.8%	4.8%	39.4%
33.7	37.0	29.3	0.5	4.3	93.9	1.8
19.7	37.9	42.4	16.5	44.6	7.2	48.2
10.5	31.9	57.6	6.0	77.7	8.5	13.8
49.9	27.2	22.9	9.0	61.4	4.1	34.5
45.5	31.5	23.0	17.9	51.4	4.3	44.3
30.8	37.8	31.4	13.5	72.5	3.4	24.1
33.3	34.8	21.9	6.7	16.0	64.2	19.8
47.5	25.8	26.7	6.3	54.0	8.7	37.3
12.2	27.4	60.4	13.9	44.8	39.5	15.7
20.9	34.3	44.8	10.0	4.4	93.4	2.2
15.3	40.9	33.8	6.3	46.4	4.4	49.2
11.4	35.9	52.7	12.1	95.7	1.1	3.2
25.0	40.4	34.6	2.4	80.3	12.6	7.1
15.6	43.7	40.7	9.1	46.4	5.1	48.5
52.7	25.9	21.4	16.0	36.6	37.3	26.1
27.3	24.2	48.5	3.5	43.9	6.2	49.9
33.7	37.8	28.5	14.8	56.7	3.5	39.8
27.7	38.5	33.8	16.0	58.5	4.0	37.5
18.4	34.5	47.1	11.7	73.8	3.1	23.1
45.4	29.8	24.8	8.5	48.0	20.4	31.6
23.9	36.4	39.7	6.2	42.8	8.5	48.7

Index

186